UWA HU

Why Donald Trump?

The Alpha Ink, LLC
Where Your Legacy Begins

Published in the United States of America

ISBN: (*sc*) 978-1-7334090-3-2
          (*e*) 978-1-7334090-4-9

1. Poetry
2. Political Science
19.06.04

I dedicate this work to all mankind in pursuance of true progress, lasting peace, freedom and love for every human being, in the firm belief that we are indisputably capable of changing the course of the loveless and therefore destabilising events now prevalent in our world today. This we can do by summoning and utilising our inherent Power of Love at all levels of our interactions, individually or globally, which has been totally ignored till date, at best misdirected and underestimated for a long time, all to our detriment, politically and above all, spiritually. I am therefore calling all of us to take action in bringing this about. It is high time!

A REVIEW

This work, both in its contents and literary style, makes a convincing, impressive and interesting reading, especially in the light of the current state of apparent chaos and conflict in many of the world's societies. It is a forensic and wide-ranging examination of the process in humanity (from the cradle to the grave) and the world systems, showing how our corrupted values have led to the broken and conflict-ridden societies we now have. In the author's words, "all aspects of our lives are thus corrupted and have veered away from the expectations of the lifestyles of those who are made in the likeness of the image of God..."

The poems suggests a way forward; and one to which society must finally pay heed, if current trends are to be arrested and corrected. There needs to be a recognition that God created man in his own image and that all creation can only operate harmoniously in the currency of love because, God himself is love and everything in creation is composed of God's love.

While agreeing with the writer, as a Christian, one notes that man, in his fallen state, has often found it difficult and unable to walk consistently in this kind of love. To the glory of God however, after our consistent failures through the ages, to heed the inspired messages of many enlightened men of God in all the continents, hence all the past and present global religious, economic banditry and exploitation and moral decay; finally, the teachings of Jesus Christ, the son of God himself, are meant to make it possible and easier for us not only to recognise our long-standing lives of lovelessness, but also to be able to rededicate our lives to obeying the inescapable love based on the holy and adamantine will of his father— the one God! This alone will ensure the overdue achievement of a better life on earth for all his children; no matter to what religion or race we may belong.

Ndu Udensi

CONTENTS

Part Two

Damage Control

INTRODUCTION

I will be eighty-one years old in December, a retired onetime lecturer in the performing arts, a songwriter and singer, an artist, a playwright and author.

As far as I can recall, all my works have one thing in common, namely that they all express my desire to find the real purpose for our existence here on earth.

They all ask the same questions and delve into the naturally available yet seemingly illusive answers that stare us all in the face or perhaps simply get ignored by the generality of humanity time after time.

These questions which I consider crucial to helping mankind come to grips with their common fate are:

Who am I really?
What am I doing here?
What is this place?
How am I to live in this here?

These questions may seem enigmatic but nature has abundant answers for all of us to discover and these are all around and within our purview. We only need to stop and contemplate deeply for the much-needed revelations of the well-structured workings of the primordial natural laws that govern creation in the adamantine and Holy will of The Creator.

For instance, each one of us is given a name whose meaning is meant to chaperone and pilot us through life.

Mine being Uwa [Igbo] which means 'the world' or 'the universe' and better still, 'fate'; has riddled me with much concern since childhood about my life and that of humanity at large [in my 'world' as it were]. It has compelled me to engage myself in the effort spiritually and artistically to find out what life is all about and to come to understand who we really are, leading to my writing of the work entitled *The Love That We Are* subtitled 'Our True Identity', to be found in major book outlets like Amazon, Barnes and Noble and the like.

I was guided in this effort by my experiences and greatly enlightened by a most lucid, indisputable and comprehensive work on all the ramifications of all existence in relation to the supremacy of the Love of the originating Godhead and His adamantine Will in the Work, *In the Light of Truth: The Grail Message* by Abd-ru-shin which means the Son of Light.

One's name, said to be what one really is and one's chaperon and pilot, indicates the fact that the bringer of this Message imbues His work with His essence, making every sentence in His Message in the Will of His Father, to shine light into the spirit of man for the understanding of all aspects of life and existence in God's Creation, clarifying the Bible!

This is to enable humanity at this time to finally get rid of the darkness that has enveloped us through time from the dark radiations of our thoughts, our words and our actions in order to return the world to what it was meant to be,—a true reflection of paradise where only Love reigns in the inviolable Will of the Creator.

*The work *In the Light of Truth: The Grail Message* can be obtained from Alexander Bernhardt Publishing. USA.

This spiritual work, alone in its own class, gives all the answers to all matters of life and existence in all the known and unknown universes, visible and invisible!

PREFACE

My work here, is an exposition of fifty-nine related pieces of poetry, in two hundred and forty-three pages, expressing my perceptions of the reasons and suggestions for the reversal of the upheavals in all aspects of human existence that now persists in the world at large, prompted by my life time of observations of happenings round the world that have adversely affected humanity's ability to achieving any sustainable degree of peaceful coexistence with one another in all the world's villages, towns, cities, and countries. This sad condition is currently most evident in the present volatile and controversial happenings here at home and in other parts of the world.

The poems are in two parts:

The first part of the pieces traces and highlights the psychological, societal and cultural whys and wherefores of the mechanisms of the world's questionable prevalent political, religious, educational and social systems and processes that have undermined humanity's ability to maintaining good moral principles in the delivery of both private and public duties in any unit of the human society round the globe; pinpointing the adverse effects these have had on mankind as a whole.

The second part offers the suggestions for countering these effects and reversing the situations for now and for the future.

This is hopefully in order that humanity may at last find the sublime peace and happiness we have missed for thousands of years succeeding years of our human evolutionary journey towards the establishment of world peace. The work enjoins the reader and listener to view the events of our present-day humanity from a consciousness that aspires to see us recapture our nobler, happier and spiritually purer lifestyle for all mankind.

First Part

The Seeds

The voice of reason cries for reason in the dark
Knowing no one is listening to his heart
If it continues someone may awaken from the trance
Someone may want to stop the moaning
With a sigh of relief born of despair
Which has gripped and stripped us bare
Numbed our consciences with flare
Multiplied the bruises that keep our spirits maimed

Something inside keeps saying
That something is happening
Something is happening
Something is happening
Something is really happening brothers and sisters.
Something that sears the mind that quakes and shivers
Something extraordinary, something esoteric,
Something intrinsically toxic and symbolic!

If it were not so,
Then why, why are we so dazed?
Why are we so afraid?
Why are we so flabbergasted
Why are we so incoherent when asked
How we stand in life's battle ground
With our eyes wide and our lips bound
Our ears tuned to a cataclysmic rebound

Of that which will catapult mankind back
To that place assigned to the past
That place that sets the clock back
From progress and from peace
That no man's land of despondency
Of desolation and regret
That torturous road to fear and blame
Which man and nature cannot contain

That's why all the agitation
That's why the threatening insurrections
The hustling and rumbling
The juggling and cringing
The wagging of tongues
And the throwing of stones
The confusion and consternation
The apprehension of the–inevitable

But providence has taken an emergency step
In a monumental counter event
Putting darkness under house arrest
Forcing it to expose all its tricks for self-defense
So mankind can by them cat-scan itself
And effect the necessary damage control
And save all humanity at this end time
From the gravity of our decline

The Seeds Of Promise

We have what it takes to take the leap
Out of the ills that make our hearts bleed
For our forgotten survival creed
We have the gift to fathom what's astir
We have the gift to perceive what's in the air
For God gave us our five senses
For mastering the earth and the challenges
That we must face in achieving lasting peace

He gave us our two eyes
To see what pleases or scares
He gave us our two legs
To leap high with hope of landing safe
On firm ground not hang in mid air
He gave us our crowns of heads
To house our discerning brains
For evaluating events with appropriate concern

God gave us our two arms
For offering helping hands with open hearts
God gave us our mouths
For speaking to others with calm and charm
And eating to sustain our valiant lives
Gave us our brave hearts
To beat with Love and not with lust
As it pumps our blood to keep us strong

Gave us our two lungs
To pump the air we breathe from dusk till dawn
Gave us our tongues
To speak the truth with all resolve
Gave each a pair of ears
To hear all with good cheer
Gave us a pair of hands
To work the land to fill our barns

Gave each two strong feet
To stand, walk and explore the fields
Gave us the gift of Love
To give to the world
No matter the case
No matter the place
No matter the name
Whatever the shape

God gave each one fingers
To turn His gifts to boundless wonders
God gave each one a face
To identify and make each serve
The world in our special ways
No matter the race
No matter the gender
No matter the time and clime

No matter the dye of our skins
Or what we dream or what we think
We have His gifts right inside alike
Where our spirits reside to guide all alike
All the rest far inside alike
Where our consciences lie
To tell us what is right
Yet we often fail to act right

Displaying ill traits with ease
Forcing our good nature to recede
Trying this and that to win the rat race
Forcing all the ills to escalate
Making us conceal the good gifts
He gave all for the common goal
Of making the world a peaceful happy home
Everything veering away from the right plan

Seeds For Love

At birth we were all colour blind
We were ego blind
Were Looks blind
And status blind
Nationality blind
Were Culture blind
Demography blind
All were Politics blind
Were Religion blind

Were Race blind
Were Caste blind
We were Heritage blind
Were Rights blind
Were Gender blind
Were possession blind
Were addiction blind

Blind to fame and all it takes
Blind to hatred and all it takes
Blind to anger and all it takes
Blind to envy and all it takes
Blind to cruelty and all it takes
Blind to vanity and all it takes
Blind to power and all it takes
Blind to sex and all it takes

As a child you and I wanted to eat
You and I wanted to sleep
You and I wanted to play
You and I wanted to grow up
You and I wanted to be the star
You and I wanted a happy home
You and I didn't want to be alone
You and I throve on hope

For you and I
There was nothing but life
Nothing but just to be alive
Nothing but to laugh and cry
Nothing but to play and smile
And run around for awhile
Bringing joy to all around
Giving posterity a happy launching ground

Dreaming of a happy world
Contemplating a loving world
Wishing for an adventurous world
As you and I grew
We began to dream big dreams
As you and I grew
We wanted to fly on the wings of our dreams
To soar to the sky with our dreams

You and I never wanted to fail nor falter
You and I only wanted to conquer
You and I dreamt we could be
Anything we wanted to be
A doctor, a nurse, an astronaut, to be

An engineer, a poet, a musician, to be
An athlete, a gymnast, an artist, to be,
An architect, an inventor, a pilot and more

As a child you and I
Dreamt to be a scientist
A pharmacist
A director
A professor
A corporate boss
A designer
A farmer
A dancer

May be an actor
May be an inventor
May be a boxer
May be a chef or a writer
May be a teacher and a singer
May be a poet and a painter
May be a composer and a conductor
May be a rapper, a ruler or a soldier

As a child you and I
Did not dream to be an atheist
As a child you and I
Did not dream to be drug addicts
As a child you and I
Did not dream to be gangsters
As a child you and I
Did not dream to be mob bosses

As a child you and I
Did not dream to be murderers
As a child you and I
Did not dream to be pimps
As a child you and I
Did not dream to be armed robbers
As a child you and he or she
Did not dream to be scammers or forgers

Nor did we dream to be a thief or a liar
A whore, a pimp, a terrorist or a traitor
A beggar on the street, homeless and jobless
You and I wanted to be respected
To be valued and accepted
You and I wanted to love
You and I wanted to be loved
You and I did not want wars

Nor did we want to be orphaned
You and I wanted to make a difference
Not put our lives on the fence
But humanity has betrayed itself
And put you and I in defence
By destroying the natural bond
Of all creatures under the sun
The natural bonding of all of man born

The Original Engagement

God being Love
Who made everything out of His Love
His original ever enduring intention
Is for peace and joy in all the worlds
Brought about by the expression of Love
From man to man and all creatures in the world
Jesus Christ wished 'Peace' to the world
In every home and to everyone He met

As the personification of God's Divine Love
In His mission of Love to all the world
He resurrected the Love we buried
In our lovelessness to all the breed
Throughout all recorded history
Showing us that the only way
To fulfil His Father's adamantine Will
Is to Love God first with all our will

And to Love our neighbours as ourselves
To do unto them as we would always
Like it to be done to us ourselves
Loving our neighbours as we love ourselves
Christians, Jews, Muslims and the rest
We would want to know best
That which unites us
Not that which divides us

Loving our neighbours as we love ourselves
We would want to know best
What helps the other grow
Not what makes him unable to play his role
For mankind as a whole
We would want to know
What makes the other's life sparkle
Not what keeps him in shackles

Loving our neighbours as we love ourselves
Christians, Jews, Muslims and the rest
We would want to know best
What makes the other shine
Not what covers him in slime
We would want to supply
What makes the other thrive
Not what causes his decline

Loving our neighbours as we love ourselves
We would want to know best
What makes the other happy
Not what increases his apathy
We would want to give
What helps the other win
Not what makes him lose and cringe
Like a bird that lost its wings

Loving our neighbours as we love ourselves
Christians, Jews, Muslims and the rest
We would want to know best
What helps the other succeed

Not what makes his dreams cease
We would help each other with ease
To make the world a better place
For all inhabitants of our earth

Defection

But we have forgotten the original plan
Brushed aside all the mentoring parts
All should play in the interest of all mankind
But sought to exploit our gifts in self pride
Plundering and ceasing others wealth
With selfishness on our family crests
Everyone else in our challenging earth
Trampled down in the grabbing craze

We have turned our world upside down
Counterfeited our images of the Holy Crown
Now we look much more like clowns
Garbed in flamboyant ceremonial gowns
Mimicking each other in a suicidal dance
Like brainwashed devotees in a trance
Our saintly selves bound and gagged
Trampled down and kicked to the curb

Our egos corrupted in this remiss
Make us see the world with corrupted eyes
That see only things on the material isles
Employing all the five but less of the sixth sense
That places us on a higher sensing step
With intuitive, powerful discerning lens
A tool of the Love that composes
All human men and all human women

Like a radar it scans all actions to be
To inform us the right ways to speak
To act or not to act, to think or not to think
To do just any and everything
It alerts us from our inner psyche
But often we fail to heed its gentle voice
And shut it up with an intellectual choice
To later regret the true answer foiled

Our corrupted egos now do not care
To see the warning glares of the volcanic flares
From the mountains of our mistakes
Gathering the forces of high seismic strength
Our corrupted egos now do not listen
To that small still voice inside the prisons
We built round it with bloated images
Of self-pride fortified with self-love

Our gagged intuition not able to function
Makes it difficult to have the recognition
Nor the volition to let Love drive all our actions
Shunning all that shun its injunctions
All our behaviours and policies devoid of Love
Make us turn blind eyes
To loveless acts of all types
Implanting vices in human life styles

That make us combat with the Loving Force
That galvanised all that has taken form
With Living Love as the creative lever
Given to man for his survival in all weather
Making us subvert our own true nature
Degrading our given valour
Subjecting ourselves to squirming victims
In the palatial spread of invincible Love

The Choking Vice

The vices now hold us down
Making it difficult for us to wear our crowns
Of victory over all the throngs
Of obstacles that want to throw us down
From the pinnacles of success
In all our attempts to progress
From ignorance to the true knowledge
Of how to make our world a better place

For instance, to steal as we and our leaders do
Is a vice that goes against the nature of Love
For Love does not engender greed
But imparts contentment in its creed
In the true nature of a human being
To be cruel as we and our leaders can be
Is a vice which gives rise to suffering
And it's against the nature of Love

For Love generates kindness
In the true nature of a human being
To lie or falsify facts
As we and our leaders do is a vice
Which creates distrust and strife
And is not the nature of Love
For Love instills honesty and sincerity
In the true nature of a human being

To discriminate against anyone
As we and our leaders do is a vice
Which incites hatred and crimes
And it is not the nature of Love
For Love loves all
In the true nature of a human being
To hate anyone for anything
As we and our leaders often do is a vice

Which promotes disputes and all forms of strife
And that is not the nature of Love
For Love furthers lasting peace and joy
In the true nature of a human being
At home and abroad and everywhere we live
To be bigoted as our leaders is a vice
Which promotes hatred and pride
And those are not the natures of Love

For Love induces humility
In the true nature of a human being
To be greedy
As we and our leaders are is a notorious vice
Which promotes exploitation
That is not the nature of Love
For Love inspires altruism
In the true nature of a human being

To be violent and aggressive
As we and our leaders can be are vices
Which plague mankind with fatal crisis
That is not the nature of Love

For Love inspires peace and harmony
In the true nature of a human being
To be rude and crude
As we often are

Turn people into fools
That is not at all the nature of Love
For Love gives prudence a healthy boost
In the true nature of a human being
To be boastful
As we and our leaders can be
Is a vice anyone can easily see
It gives support to vanity

And that is not the nature of Love
For Love instills humility
In the true nature of a human being
To be divisive
As we and our leaders often are
Is a vice that prompts disunity and strife
And that is not the nature of Love
For love infuses unity

For the maintenance of harmony
In the true nature of a human being
To be despotic
As we and they can be is a vice
That sponsors oppression
Which puts progress in recession
And that is not the nature of Love
Nor the true nature of a human being

For Love propagates equality for all
Now hawked on political stalls
For the world domination race
That has overshadowed the human case
Still God gives to all alike
No matter the race, the time or clime
His Will drills both haves and have nots
In the east, west, south or north

Not restricting any gifts
Of His treasures to all that exist
With Love He provides for all to share
With the hand that is always fair
Urging man to let his input
Complete the Love based circuit
But hither and thither, we plunder
Scheming and tearing all asunder

Some folks soaring above their peers
Yet going to bed in red hot tears
Dreaming of their long-lost selves
In the maddening, breathless rat race
Yet all are equally meant to climb the mountains
To drink from life's treasure fountains
To rise to the breathtaking tops
And give thanks to God

Now the sirens blare loud and clear
In the drums of everyone's inner ears
Block not the sounds that scream and say
That we must stop new Jericho's walls

From tumbling down in a fatal fall
Letting mankind drown again in the sprawl
For we are meant to hold the fort
And break the choking vice on Love

Rekindle the transforming torch of love
And illuminate, not darken the world
For we are all committed souls
Wanting to play our natural helpful roles
In making the world a happy place
We all run the same survival race
We all now suffer the same torturing pains
Cascading down our bewildered veins

Cause our struggles now seem in vain
Yet we all are well equipped for the winding tracks
To pass Love's baton with no slack
From hand to hand
From track to track
To red, black, white or yellow
Lighting the paths for all to follow
Strong and bold to win the race

And join hands with smiles on our faces
But man has sabotaged his own survival game
And put you and I in constant defence
By destroying the protective strength
Of the natural bonding of man with man
Between one neighbour and another
One clan and another
One social group and another

One political group and another
One religious group and another
The family bond too hangs on the balance
Cause family members are lost in the avalanche
Of the war of the survival of the fittest
There is little love now lost in the tempest
Between one political party and another
Between one nation and the other

Bombastic plots and counter plots are hatched
To make the world a battle ground
Of bedazzled antelopes staggering around
Stumbling weak-kneed with our dreams
Groping for water in the foaming seas
Glimpsed through tinted political and religious screens
That contort, and distort every scene
Demonising and trivialising everything gleaned

Destroying the reality of sanity,
Compelled to step on each other's toes
Or strike each other down with bigoted blows
Because the dreams we had faded in the haze
Driving us to fabricate and castigate,
Degrade, humiliate and intimidate
Each other in the recurring fight
To regain our lost human rights

Seeds Of Discord

Tomorrow is now dark and blank
Nothing satisfying the struggling man
Anxious to break the invisible hand
That holds him back
From taking firm stands and making plans
To escape from our self-made traps
But remember we have the gifts
To self-release all traps with ease

For we set the traps by seizing all nature's yields
Panting with unabated greed
That has set the world burning with its seeds
We set the traps
By making and breaking people feeling smug
That has made the world insensitive to wars
We set the traps
With hate and prejudice yielding all the crimes

Now we grope around and thrash about
We look around and move around
Here, there and everywhere
Nothing seeming to calm our rattling nerves
Nothing soothing the gnawing pains
Nothing healing the gaping wounds
In the wombs of aspiring youths
Of bruised humanity

We look up
We look down
Our heads low and our hands down
It seems we are beaten
Our faces grim as we cling
With bated breath and clenched fists
Onto the staggering weight of tomorrow
Knowing not what will follow

Are we still fit for the survival race
When all that we can trace
Haven't helped us win the case
Of what makes us consciously break
Our sacred bonds at birth with mother earth
And cast gloomy shadows on our lives
Making us wish we were never born
To reap what we have sown

The problems we have all now contrived
Stem from our over the top self-pride
Bagged with the claim of the superiority
Of strands of favoured humanity
Precipitating all the strife
That have plagued mankind
From time to time
And clime to clime

But all were created equal
All are meant to feel equal
Contradicting this holy edict
In various manmade cliques

Has shot-circuited progress
In all human developmental processes
And fanned the raging flame
Of discrimination with all its attendant banes

Stoking the fumes of oppression
In all fields of human aspiration
The Napoleonic and Hitlerian complexes
Resurge here and there unabated
In the world's heads of states
Cast in those same vain moulds
With egos out of control
Oblivious of the turmoil they unfold

For why do we want to know
Who is black and who is not
If not to break the natural bond
And divide and rule the clinging mob
Why do we want to know
Who is brown and who is not
If not to diffuse the sublime union
And plant separatism as a winning ruse

In a brazen show of power abuse
A jaundiced attempt at isolation
Which contradicts the bonds of cooperation
That links one human to the other
In the never ebbing sea of everlasting Love
A blatant, senseless seizure of power
From the gentle hands of the power of Love
That formed and governs all that exist.

The Menace Of Racism

Now racism has reared its head
And set the mark for winning the race
For freedom and equality of all the human race
Carrying the baton for discourses
In politics, religion, economy and what nots
Forcing us to bargain with our looks
And be bound to be misunderstood
Simply by the colours of our hoods

But underneath the skin all is red flesh
Nothing but red and white blood cells
Under the skin there are just bones
Nothing but bones and more bones
Under the skin there are the veins
Nothing but veins and billions of veins
Under the skin there are arteries
Nothing but arteries and all those are the same

All the same right to the end
The names of the bones are the same
The names of the organs are the same
The names of the fluids are the same
The white, the red cells look the same
Their sizes and functions are the same
All regenerate and degenerate
All consummate the human race

No one race works better than the other
No one race thinks better than the other
No one race sees better than the other
No one race knows more than the other
No one race is more gifted than the other
No one race aims higher than the other
All human beings are meant to join hands
In the bid for progress for all mankind

The D.N.A's Trumpet

All of us are the same in the core
It does not matter
That he is white and feels superior
And I am not and feel underrated
We are all created in the same Likeness
Of the Image of God's Loving essence
Having the same burning aspirations
To do our best in differing locations

Though our geographical locations
Have induced significant anatomical variations
In the wake of the human evolution
Necessity the mother of inventions
Imposed necessary variations
In the human evolutionary adaptation
To different weather conditions
In the differing locations

From the north to the south
From the east to the west
Our world has organically imposed on us
The features most practical for success
In navigating the environments of our births
From the equator to the tropic of Cancer
And the Capricorn to the Poles
From the torrid to the frigid zones

Nature let us evolve characteristic features
That adequately help us successfully cope
With the weather effects on our survival codes
Those in the equatorial zone of the earth
In the middle of the north and South of the earth
And those in the tropics flanking them
Are blessed with the abundance of God's gifts
Some with the colour of skins so rich
They need no more tanning nor bleach

Pampered with abundant flora
Adorned with enchanting fauna
And protected with the body types
That shield them from the sun in the sky
And the precipitations of heat and rain
With wooly hairs to cover their heads
Wide nostrils for the weighty humid air
Wide thicker lips for making sounds

To pierce their heavy atmospheric bounds
Abundant fruits from nature's barns
To pick and nourish bodies and minds
With gratitude to the benevolent source
If it were not for decorum and for fun
They barely needed any body accoutrements
As do the inhabitants in the challenging environments
Of other primates who migrated further away

From the warmth of the abundant sun rays
In this evolutionary march of the human race
They too evolved the necessary body types
To protect them from the harsher weather bites

The skins becoming lighter and lighter
Adjusting to the much colder weathers
Adapting to the less humid conditions
Of the southern, sunnier weather emanations

Nose bridges became much higher
Their nostrils became much narrower
To insulate their breath now much colder
Necessity the mother of invention
Forced their hands to device solutions
To their life-threatening weather conditions
Foot wears to prevent frost bites
Clothings to prevent hypothermia

Other inventions following in this quest
To augment the human survival kits
One thing leading to another ever since
Our imitation of one another unabridged
Has led us to the raging rat race
That is now strangling the human race
From the north to the southern poles
From the east to the western coasts

Our needs are meant to force our hands
In deducing the relevant steps to take
In every adverse developmental stage
And invent the relevant means
Of unlocking the treasures within
The different races of human beings
That we may all make our contributions
To our ever evolving civilisation

The world cannot fulfil this obligation
When one man prevents the other man
From giving his/her gift in the universal plan
When one race prevents the other race
From adding their unique gifts to the chase
For the unification of diversity in mutual inclusions
For the overall success and satisfaction
Of all peoples in God's Creation

No matter the specifics of our breed
No matter the culture nor the creed
Nor the specific zones of our birth
All bear the same responsibilities
All face the same heavenly call
And when we lay down our human overalls
We do not go to any heavenly 'race' balls
The goose and the gander share the same stall

Clamouring Dreams

We all have the same questions to answer
When all is over and done sooner or later
Nature is founded on the Divine radiations
Of God's Love particles in perfection
Man as part of that perfection
Is meant to retain the perfection
In rigorous physical employment
Of all his benevolent endowments

Clamouring for manifestations
In every human male and human female
So it does not matter
If he is tall and looks secure
And I am short and self-conscious
Each size is right for the special task
Of taking care of special mankind's plight
So give him and I the chance to try

For we all have the same questions to answer
When all is over and done sooner or later
It does not therefore matter
If she is pretty and admired
And I am not and ignored
Each with our looks have a role to play
In making the world a happy place
No matter the race, no matter the case

So give both of us the chances to try
For we all have the same questions to answer
When all is over and done sooner or later
It does not therefore matter
That he is popular and influential
And I am not recognised by the media
The rule is to win each other's love
By loving the other as we love ourselves

So give both of us the chances to try
We all have the same questions to answer
When all is over and done sooner or later
It does not therefore matter
That he is successful and I am not
The measure of success is not in gold
But in our efforts to serve God's household
With the talents in our control

So give us the chances to try
We all have the same questions to answer
When all is over and done sooner or later
Our leaders and us have material clouts
But strength is based on integrity
And the ability to empower humanity
With the best of our abilities
So give all the chances to try

We all have the same questions to answer
When all is over and done sooner or later
It does not therefore matter
That they are rich men and we are paupers

The truly rich have giving hearts
For the more we give
The more we will receive
So give all the chances to try

For we all have the same questions to answer
When all is over and done sooner or later
It does not therefore matter
If we are rulers
And are served hand and foot
And others are our subjects
To serve us hand and foot
Both are required to serve each other with Love

So give all the chances to try
We all have the same questions to answer
When all is over and done sooner or later
It does not therefore matter
If we are the bosses
And others are the ones
At the bottom of the rungs
Do to others as we would want done to us

So give all the chances to try
To bring out our given treasures
To share with every one with pleasure
Joining hands with Mother Nature
To make the world a happy place
As it was meant in the very first place
By the Creator of all the human race
With the Love that governs the universe

The Chameleon Spell

The original plan of living with Love
With our natural gifts for living with Love
Are under the siege of callousness
That has seized the human consciousness
Reversing our natural aptitudes for Loving
From colour blindness to colour phobia
Nationality blindness to xenophobia
Status blindness to status hunting

Selflessness to selfishness
Image blindness to vanity
Religion blindness to spiritual banditry
Cultural blindness to acculturation
Political blindness to ideological masturbation
Race blindness to crass racism
Caste or clan blindness to tribalism
Pride blindness to narcissism

Power blindness to megalomania
Hatred blindness to war mongering
Anger blindness to irritability
Envy blindness to jealousy
Cruelty blindness to war and insensitivity
We point fingers at each other and gesticulate
Shaking our heads as we pontificate
Railing over this, that and the other

Not blaming selves but only others
Crowding our days with crucibles of doom
Reaching out for sympathy in our gloom
Painting black white
Or the other way around
Whichever delights or wins the fights
Even if we die in the lies
Changing camps at will in the sly

Instead of the real us made with Love
That should only act with love
Our demonised egos have become cruel
Making others writhe in mortal pain
While we bask in pleasure and fame
Instead of the real us
That should only act with Love
Our distorted egos discriminate

Creating false images of ourselves
Claiming rights we deny everyone else
Shattering the blueprint of God's Love
Instead of the real us
That should always give help
Our distorted egos have become possessive
Cramping goodness in a cage of thorns
Leaving no room in our hearts to reform

Instead of the real us
That should only act with Grace
The baseness of our distorted egos
Has made us rude and crude

Mindless of the trailing bruises
That has turned us into brutes
Leaving prudence in the lurch
Smearing dung on the face of Love

Instead of the real us
That should always be content
Our distorted egos now salivate with greed
Acquiring much more than we can ever need
Hoarding and cluttering our homes with goods
Most of which do no good
Devising means to accumulate more
Looting resources from many shores

In place of the real us
That should shun pride
Our distorted egos take high horses rides
Hunting for pomp and glory
Instead of donkey riding in Christlike humility
In place of the real us
That should only act with Love
Our distorted egos have become prejudiced

Fanning discontent, making enemies
Upsetting the law of nature's equity
Instead of the real us
That should always speak the truth
And nothing but the truth
Our distorted egos bend the truth
To help us run away
From facing the shame we deserve

Instead of the real us
That should only act with Love
Our distorted egos
Wanting to gain control
Of the centre we cannot hold
Divide the household
Melting down communal moulds
Setting one group against the other

Instead of the real us
That should be kind and generous
Our distorted egos become nepotistic
Transformed into cackling human hens
Nesting only our family chicks
Pecking at those that don't belong
To the coop secured by family bonds
Or sworn to the oaths of fraternity songs

Instead of the real us
That should only espouse peace
Our distorted egos take to violence
With the patronage of hate
Giving way to wild emotions
Coursing through us in wild confusion
Making us lose the will to resolve
And solve all our ills with Love

In place of the real us
That should only live with love
Our distorted egos in power lust
Crack the whip of oppression

Propping our weak dispositions
In our unfit intentions to rule the nations
With our uncouth disregard
Of living and letting others live

All the above traits
Have woven a virus laden nest
Of returning boomerangs in a basketful of snakes
Delivered by those who bear the badge of honour
Conferred to them with pomp and grandeur
In the valour of our fervour
For a people get the leaders they favour
In Africa, Australia, or Antartica,

Asia, Europe or old Babylonia
The Egyptians, Incas and Aztecs and Indians
And all our ancestors, ancient and modern
From the east to the west of the globe
From the north to the south of the pole
There are no mitigations, no exceptions
No variations, no exclusions
Because Love has not been in constant expression

The Cloned Seeds

The seed each of us has sown
Has born fruits for us to taste
The onetime seeds have become trees
Bursting with their characteristic breeds
Our acorns have become oaks
With branches we cannot control
And foliages spread and profuse
Casting their shades over all other shoots

Struggling to bask in the sunshine too
The oaks coarse barks became impenetrable
Their girded trunks expansive and unshakable
Their contorted roots scouring the earth
Scavenging, excavating with tooth and nail
Bent on devouring all the feeds
Meant for them and all the other trees
Dominating all the other breeds

Leaving us to find ways and means
To deal with the choking scene
The acorns we planted years ago
Without a thought but much bravado
Have become big problems for us to swallow
The profusion of the oaks' outputs
Of fruits and leaves and tap roots
Amplify the wrong steps we took

By spilling acorns on our public lawns
Our leaders are those oaks on those lawns
Displaying yields of fruits from our hands
Everything they do without care
Showcase the things we do without care
For us to see and judge ourselves
Everything they say mirror what we say
For us to hear and pinch our ears

Like them we put others in bad lights
So we can be in spotlights
Like them we condone dishonesty
Flaunt all forms of immodesty
With blatant complacency
At work or play,
Night and day
At home or abroad

We wade in mud and smear our shoes
And think no one can see the clues
But the ears of time hear the chilling blues
In the heat of that which is fuming
Casting grotesque shadows spewing
Out from Aladdin's lamp
With claws full of contrabands
Swindled from the homeland

All these unceasing throes
Give steam to the upsurging flow
Of need for actions in our quests
To retrieve our golden dream eggs

Snatched from our nests
With commercialised political dexterity
Hawked in the markets of immorality
And in the barns of greed

That crisscross oceans to make inhumane deals
All through the industrial grids and grain fields
The hands with which our industrialist shake
Are often smeared with slippery grease
From coasts of lands that fuel our greed
Consumers become door mats
Often are the punching bags
When stock markets are on the slack

Our leaders planning and strategising
Buttering no other but friends with might
Turning around and biting the hands
That unwittingly feed their pride
Making us true lookalikes not otherwise
Ramping up each other's flaws
By failing to hear the ominous tones
Of the poor man's moans

They fail to give back like us
They fail to see their faults like us
They fail to be kind like us
They fail to forgive like us
They fail to help like us
They fail to respect like us
They fail to be truthful like us
They fail —— to Love!

Like them we don't hear
The trembling and foreboding blare
In the sobbing of the broken hearted
The sighing of the tender hearted
The dirge of the forgotten
The agitation of the downtrodden
The rebellious cry of the oppressed
The aggression of the suppressed

The prudent in this callous mimicry
Has no succour in the face of the infantry
Of wealth and suppressive grandeur
Money is the haloed god of all it lures
A good friend to cover up and shield
The wounded hearts of those who bleed
From neglects and regrets they cannot trash
But are safely concealed in investment banks

Like them we often fail to see the gale ahead
Nor our golden limousines roofs agape
As we cruise through our gilded gates
Cause the shins on them are so bright
That they dazzle and singe our eyes
And our heads spin to the euphoric pivoting
Into byways and detours that have juggled our fates
And turned us now into seasoned marauders

Like them many times we fail
To put ourselves in restraint
Fail to curb our desires
That seem so much to inspire our pride

And fire our over ambitious strides
So many times we both fail to heed
The cries of people in grief
Many times fail to look at the glaring grins

Of men, women and children
That line the streets in the pain
That has chiseled their frozen manes
And labeled them abandoned,
Branded them as the forbidden
Classified them as the forgotten
In the lands of milk and honey
The lands of dreams and bounties

Like them we tend to milk other's cows
But secure our own and our houses
Cry wolf where there are only horses
Place heavy hands on shoulders
That lean on broken boulders
Saying it is not our business
To love others as we love ourselves
Nor do unto others as we would want done to us

But the ringing in our ears
Raise the ears of wandering deers
Saying that something is now afoot
That we should turn around and take a look
And fix the leaks in the tires
Of our thread-worn lives
That the fog ahead may becloud our end
That it is vain to stagger ahead heads bent

With nothing but dreams of shelters
And some bread at the end of the chase
That we are floating in a high centigrade
Of a self-induced hurricane
Where the winds of fate are stronger than our wills
And our guts nutted by these dreadful drills
That we are brutalised and de-sensitised
Dehumanised, destabilised and demoralised

How are the mighty so fallen?
We seem to have given up the fight
To Tom, Dick and uncle Harry
With all the pomp and all the glory
Who care not for any of the story
And like them, with little or no worry
Say one thing and mean another
Baring our teeth in fake smiles

The Lord Jesus had said:
"Let your yea be yea
And your nay be nay"
Or are we not the Christians we tout so loud
In the "One Nation under God" as all nations should
Are we not true Muslims or true Jews
Are we not true Hindus and Buddhists too
All religions extol the same moral creed

Mirror Mirror On The Wall

Mirror mirror on the wall
Tell the truth to us all
Are we not all lions in sheep skins
Like our leaders, the same old hypocrites
Make us remember the depths to which we sunk
With our deeds in times of need:
Those devious and pernicious deeds
Those selfish and pretentious deeds

Those deceitful deeds
Those acrimonious deed
Cause no one was looking
So we thought
No one was probing
So it seemed
No one counting
So we thought

No one chastising
So it seemed
Not even our consciences
Not even our lip-serving avowal
Of chastity and religiosity
Nothing could arrest our declining humanity
We jogged along with robotic ardor
Geared to burst our veins in wild pursuits of pleasure

Sparing nothing, caring for no one but self
Always insatiable, in want and desperation
Always in the embrace of clannish idiosyncrasies
In the slipperiness of crass hypocrisy
Plots and counter plots piggy-backing greed,
Crass manipulations on the horse backs of jealousy
The tricky monkey of envy
The conniving serpent of deceit

You name it, we have all done it—
Our chosen leaders are our true mirrors indeed
Ah, could we but learn from the bodies
Exhumed from their vaults!
Like them we do whatever it takes
To advance our stakes
Like them we exaggerate
Like them we vilify others

But glorify ourselves and ours
Like them we dominate the other
Like them we intimidate the other
All these perjure our individual souls
We justify our deeds with might
We undermine the other in the sly
Avoiding the challenges of a fair fight
Like them we shrink from giving praise

Because the other is not of our race
Is not the same in looks and achievements
In colour of skin not like us
In wealth and fame not like us

In education and class, not like us.
Not one of our friends nor our mate
Does not play the same game
Does not belong to our clan
Does not belong to our club
Does not belong to our religion
Does not speak our tongue
Not our peer, nor above all, our race!
We shrink from giving help
Because we rate the others indolent
And place ourselves above their kind
We no more know what honour is like

Cause we cannot count our daily lies
And cannot count our loveless thoughts
Cannot count our loveless words
Nor can we our loveless deeds
That have turned us all into freaks
And so do our eloquent, roving eyes,
Our gestures and the poses we strike
Glibly wagging our lies fed tongues

We lie in court,
We lie at work
We lie at play
At night or day
We lie to deceive
With so much ease
We spin rhetorics that incite
Causing friends to fight

We lie in bed with our feet in flight
And blame the other when we fail
To make our own ships sail
We get possessive and obsessive

Which turn to oppression and suppression
We are divisive and abusive
We are manipulative, deceptive and more
Callousness has run a mock

This lovelessness in our stewardship
Handcuffing all man's aspirations
For the fulfilment of God's Love intensions
For His creatures made with Love
Seem to echo thunderously
In the current leaders of our nations
The grand effigies of our reflections
Who now loom over our destiny

With pride bred in calumny
Like them we are gold diggers
Doing everything it may require
Sparing nothing, fearing nothing
Defying reason, confounding dignity,
Renegading sobriety and morality to infamy
We aid and abate with little concern
Instigate and dictate to keep the rein

Like them we make things go our way
Come shine, come rain
Come life, come death
And even hell!

Now the boomerangs have come home
Bellowing with uncanny tones
Now we wish the sun would dry our eyes
Of tears of groans in dark isle

Our racing hearts calmed and our faces bright
With laughter not with nervous smiles
Good winds of fate to blow our ways once again
With showers of soothing rains once again
From long forgotten days of grace
Crowned by the sacrifices we made
Sacrifices made by nobler hands
Drawn in the sands of time in our lands

We cannot help but remember
The joy we felt even when we blundered
Now regrets gore our hearts
With so much longing that it hurts
Right through to our growling guts
From the ulcers of the political stunts
That failed to gain the much-needed trust
In the politicians of our choice

Our heads up in a curios tilt
Hearing the punches of dissonant pitches
As we change the shifts
And drift from coast to coast
In our nightmare of political floats
Our leaders fevered ploys
Have become empty and spoilt
Turning their patriotism into nationalism

Plunging us into righteous bitterness
In our political and religious wilderness
With no clear vision of the road ahead
Bombshells of warning sirens blare
Announcing bigotry and prejudice in every flare
In every rally and every fair
Stamping our conniving messages
On the blades of the assailing boomerangs

Mirror, mirror on the wall
Mirror, mirror on the wall
Which one of us is better than the other
Is it us or they who wear red feathers
On their flamboyant hats
Is it us or they who are the executors
Of our private adventures
Our chosen edifying scape goats

Who inflicted these on us
But our mutated conniving selves
We are the ones who initiated the slide
And dismantled the creed of decency and honesty
Right before the gaze of our inherent humanity
We supplanted the sublime peaceful cause
With stunting forces of discord
Undermining genuineness and prompting the fall

Gagging the innocent and misleading the young
To whom we owe the duty to mentor
In the plan of like mother like daughter
Like father like son

We turned round and round like woollen balls
And spun yarns that choke our own guts
Making us compete with animals in aborted heats
By ignoring God's everlasting Loving scheme

Day after day we close our ears
To the cacophony of heart-rending screams
Seeping into our ears from unfulfilled dreams
Clouding our minds with untold fears
Yet brush them off as if they were never heard
Strutting about with heads held high
Pushing aside the little voice inside
Stifling lingering vestiges of the virtuous cries

Of those made in the Likeness of the Image of God
In the automatic act of the Source of all life
Though all things embody God's Love
Man alone bears the likeness of the Image of God
A benevolent act that imparts to man
The necessary attributes of Love he needs
To fulfil the strict demands
Of the Love mechanisms of the universe

These attributes encapsulate
All that is benevolent
All that is magnanimous
All that is humane
All that is pure
All that is noble and truthful
All that is kind and gentle
All that is simply good in every way

The Image Swap

But are we still the likenesses of the Image of God
Or more like those of our leaders and they like us
Trumpeting our bloated egos
Blustering our wimpy wits
From the gutters of deceit
Are we still the likenesses of the Image of God
Or more like those of our leaders and they like us
Propping our pride with the spoils of greed

Are we still the likenesses of the Image of God
Or more like those of our leaders and they like us
Washing our linens seemingly clean
By cremating our consciences
At the alter of deceit
The sepulchre of conceit
The cathedral of opulence
And the armoury of defences

In the jungle policy of might is right
How else is it that we go with our eyes blind
To the needs of our neighbours in all our streets
When we are enjoined no matter our creed
To Love them as we love ourselves
How else is it that we forget
It is better to give and receive than to extort
From the poor to dress our resorts

Are we still in the likenesses of the Image of God
Or more like those of our leaders and they like us
When we snatch the purses from the weak
Grab the reigns from the hands of champions
Discourage and disparage others
Confuse the simple minded with platitudes
That falsify our intents, perfecting our camouflages
With offers of occasional largesses

Are we still the likenesses of the Image of God
Or more like those of our leaders and they like us
When we wave our hands in public
But cringe inside with hatred
Are we still the likenesses of the Image of God
Or more like those of our leaders and they like us
When we cover up our indiscretions
Under the glittering veneer of our acquisitions

Are we now not strong-up bands of deviants
In the Likeness of our heads of states
And they in our mutated deviant states
For we both go with our eyes averted
And our minds firmly blocked
To the needs of our neighbours
When we are all enjoined to endeavour
To do good to one another

We both don't seem to remember
That we are sowing seeds for tomorrow
Everyday we live in the borough
Of He Whose Image our likenesses should be

Bringing in its wake regrets and loss of sleep
As the tortured minds of indiscretion
Stretch to breaking points with apprehension
Of what would be our future portions

For not a day is ushered
With a coherent choir of voices
Expressing their love with ardour
With good will to men of all colours
As those made in the true honour
Of God's image should endeavour
In our pledges to Him in humble homage
With unwavering obedience from age to age

In allegiance to His Holy Name
Should we then not stop
Topping the scale in breaking His rules
By dismantling natural and societal norms
Wheeling and dealing
Stealing and preening like peacocks in heat
Contracting backhanded deals
Unfitting for the likenesses of the Image of God

In the likeness of God's image
Should we rage on the road cursing and swearing,
Shooting and killing blaming others
Never accepting we may be the offenders
Never attempting to make things better
By sending good thoughts to the offender
For one good deed attracts another
In the fitting likenesses of the Image of God

But in the likeness of our leaders
We never tire of pointing fingers
Oblivious that the other three are facing us!
Cause what goes around comes around
No matter how gaudy our crowns
In the likeness of our leaders
Our hides are thicker than the crocodiles'
Our tongues sharper than razor blades

In the likeness of our leaders
We have no qualms about doing wrong
Neither do we of what makes people frown
We insinuate to implicate others
Misinform to complicate matters
We seem not to worry
So long as we make money and have buddies
Leaving our consciences marooned with apathy

What went around has come around
The boomerang touching our ground
Making much dreaded uncanny sounds
With fruits of their own dreaded kinds
Bluffing, blundering, plundering, killing
Smothering our hopes and dreams
With lies, prejudice and intimidation,
Hatred, fears and humiliations

Clearly outstripping our good contributions
Exposing our senses of mock superiority
Our double dealings to insulate our notoriety
The garnishing of our breads with honey and spice

While others gather crumbs from sties
Posturing futures secured in heaven
By the amount of money we have given
Paying the toll for our highways to heaven

Sidetracking all the cardinal rules
To ensure our common good
One of which is we should not lie!
But the husband lies
The wife lies
The children lie
The friend lies
The enemies lie

The master lies
The servant lies
The company lies
The manager lies
The employee lies
The banks lie
The manufacturers lie
The industrialists lie

The policemen lie
The lawyers lie
Religious leaders lie
Our rulers lie
At some point or another we all lie
An unworthy act in God's Holy sight
The reaping of whose fruits is not forestalled
Our boomerangs bearing the writings on our walls

The Collective Amnesia

Our mirrors on the wall
Reflect the prevalent pictures of our downfall
In the collective amnesia
Of all our required sacred duties
As the likenesses of the Image of God
Streaming the dangerous manifestos
That we must repeal and repel
So we can fuel and not be compelled

To give up our human rights
And stay contented with flimsy bites
Of our freedom of mind, power and life
As likenesses of the Image of God
In the collective amnesia
Of those required sacred duties
Of not being gagged from speaking out for humanity
Drowning in false political expediencies

Or being blinded by the touting of the deeds
Of acclaimed heroes of nationalism
In exchange for patriotism
At the expense of lasting humanism
And the quest for global harmony
In the collective amnesia
Of our inherent magnanimity
As the likenesses of the Image of God

Neither be fooled by champions of prosperity
At the expense of humility and honesty
And the decree of uprightness
In the collective amnesia
Of the maintenance of human integrity
As the likenesses of the Image of God
The mirror reflections on our walls
Further reveal the aggressive streaks

Of our lust for power and life consuming greed
In the collective amnesia
Of contented peace
As likenesses of the Image of God
Plunging mankind into uncontrollable broils
From age to succeeding ages
The mirrors again reveal
The tests we can hardly resist

Of jumping on to band wagons
Of anything that can assist
In crowning us with worldly crowns
Choosing not to be bound by morality
In the collective amnesia
Of upheld nobility
As likenesses of the Image of God
That gives man the magic rod

That manifests all he ever needs
The mirrors further reveal
Our insistent phobias and bigotry
In the collective amnesia

Of maintaining racial and social equality
As likenesses of the Image of God
Precipitating discontent and inferiority complexes
Detrimental to the progress of all the races

They reveal our hypocrisies
Rising hatred and prejudices
In the collective amnesia
Of Love, pervasive Love for all
As the likenesses of the Image of God
Prompting recurring acts
Of man's inhumanity to man—
For all around the shards do not match the pot

All we see is the rabid grip of xenophobia
Of the constant displays of all the manias
In the effects of our collective amnesias
One nation under God
Is now one nation in a fog
One nation under God
Is a wow we should all keep
Yet in this we fail to fulfil the noble dream

Dragging our future along muddy streams
We fail in economic structures
That ravage the have-nots futures
Killing their virgin dreams of success
Stifling their contributions to our progress
Shoving them to the back of life's seats
Crippling their efforts to compete
In sharing nature's bountiful feast

We fail in our relationships with one another
On our streets or neighbours across the boarder
In our homes, towns and villages
Our workplaces and our fun places
With one creed and the other
One political group and another
One tribe and another
One institution and another

One family and another
Not understanding one another
Fanning our hatred of one another
In place of our love for one another
In the collective amnesia
Of Love for all
As the likenesses of the Image of God
Causing hate groups to rise within our borders

Rebellions, terrorism, vandalism, wars
Destabilising the organic interchange
Of good will among men and in its wake
Ballooning our stress in the strifes we engage
In the collective amnesia
Of maintaining peace among our fellowmen
Harmony, brotherliness and tranquility
As the likenesses of the Image of God

Precipitating the inevitability
Of man-made and natural adversities
That now relentlessly ravage all humanity
Rapping frantically at our consciences

Nudging us to awaken from the stupor
Of our collective amnesia of universal Love
Causing discrimination and the validation
Of none ethical paradigms

Of the superiority of one race over another
One nation over another
One tribe over another
One clan over another
One class over another
One man over another
One gender over another
Reconstituting nature's nature

With hubristic beliefs in our own powers
While drifting on sinking sands of defiance
Helpless and hopeless denials
Choking with blunt disdain
Of anything plain and sane
That does not spring from our fevered brains
Our overblown egos
And our overwrought nerves

We cannot see beyond our dreams of fame
That make us ignore the breaking bones
The drooping eyes of those without homes
The deprived and degraded fellow folks
With whom we share the world
We claim we have the ways with all
To make grass grow on frozen ice
With all that science can device

We boast of having the knowledge
To change the world, turning grass to gold
Water to bread, earth to heaven ten-fold
We know it all and think we can do it all
But fail to employ the simplest tool that can do it all— LOVE—
Living Love!
The Love with which we all are made
In the likeness of God's own Image

The Social Cancer

We slander and murder
When we should praise and protect
In the way of the Love that we are
We assassinate others' characters
When we should adulate to encourage
In the way of the Love that we are
We cheat at whim even when we sleep
Against the way of the Love that we are

We cheat our wives
Against the way of Love
We cheat our husbands
Against the way of Love
We cheat our friends
Against the way of Love
We cheat our companies
Against the practice of Love

We cheat the state
Against the way of Living Love
We falsify our tax returns
Against the rules of Living Love
We solicit for donations for organisations
With fraudulent intentions
Instigated by unbridled greed
Against the ways of Living Love

We register companies that don't exist
A screaming sign of corruption
Ignoring the way of Living Love
We claim dependents that don't exist
A blatant show of dishonesty
Ignoring the way of Living Love
We falsify our earnings without remorse
To magnify our income tax returns

Ignoring the way of living Love
We hire lawyers to defend our crimes
They twist the truth with legal rhymes
That offer us alternative truths
Ignoring the Living Love rules
We meddle with others' lives
With marked insensitivity and style
Ignoring the rules of Love

We manipulate with cunning grace
Sidetracking what Love dictates
And claim trophies undeserved
To boost our egos nonetheless
Denying the rules of Living Love
Casting our fates with reckless abandon
In collision with the brandishing blades
Of our returning boomerangs

We forget that God is Love!
And formed all things out of That love
Did He discriminate for us to imitate
Did He make some races fake

Or failed to give them a favoured place
But placed their lives at stake
Then why the scrambling
Why the grumbling

Why the wrangling
Why the angling and grabbing
Why the hyperbolic flare of words reverberating
The impregnated desire to breed
Desperation, confusion with no ease
In the hyped arena of the survival of the fittest
Why the rattling of broken bones
Before the eyes of freedom fighters

And the clamour for induction nevertheless
Into the wild circles of lions in sheep skins
Why drown the other in tears from wounds
Revived while singing the blues
With scars that will not heal nor fade
But resurrect from age to age
Through subways of pent emotions
And highways of dreamt redemption—

Raise your drooping heads all peoples
Brace yourselves and shake fates hands
The boomerang stares us boldly in the face
It is time to shear the weeds we bred
It is time to stop our dances to the beat of Hate
And dance to the beat of Love
Changing the rhythm to that of healing Love
To heal our world of all political and moral flaws

The Incipient Masochism

Long have we played games with fate
Betting on power not Love to win the race
Long have we punctured the sails
On boats that ferry those whose fortunes failed
Long have we stolen the rights of the meek
Long have we plundered the barns of the weak
With equanimity and the bravado
Of the conquistadors lacking Love

Long has there been no end
To the jungle prima facie elements
Of racial discrimination in work places
In gyms, schools and fun places
In employments, education and housing places
In health giving and school funding places
In project allocations and contracting places
In job prospecting and hiring places

Discrimination against women persist
Discrimination against gays persist
Discrimination against races persist
Discrimination against tribes persist
Discrimination against clans persists
Discrimination against this or that persist
Simply because we don't want things certain ways
Simply because we prefer things our own ways

We circulate only among our kinds
And breathe our air perfumed and refined
Our piqued noses up in the air as we pose
Glaring and sneering at whom we stole
The religious digging into cramping holes
Fervently looking for rescuing hands
To drag them out from the sinking sand
Of misplaced trust on faked doctrinal hosts

How many times have we stooped low
To pull the carpet from under the feet
Of others because of our failed dreams
How often do we stoop down to be
With those not on the bill-board
Who do not have the way with all
To grease our sweaty hands
Or kiss our messy behinds

Our eyes bulging at what others found
Even though we may have mounds
Of what make some others scrounge
Our insecurity driving us round the bend
Forcing us to triple our strengths
In securing what we deem will do best
In making us more content
Greed takes over in these attempts

Clouding our senses of shame
Spurring us to play any game
That steers our marauding ships to fame
Propelled by steamy stormy gales

Women wanting more clothes
To keep their self-esteem in vogue
Women wanting more shoes
To give their styles some cheeky boost

Women wanting more jewelries
Embellishing other alluring accessories
Women wanting more coquetry,
To gloss over their inadequacies
Women wanting more flatteries
To boost their lacking femininity
Loosing their powers and sense of shame
Their integrity and the nobility of the woman's mane

Men wanting more expensive cars
To exhibit their vain financial class
Men wanting more women or partners
To satiate their overactive carnal drives
In place of their somber parental strives
Men wanting more money
To fund their egotistic hobbies
Of dangerous sports and games

Disrupting homes, endangering lives
We both wanting the fripperies of life
To distract us from the painful truth
That the end is more than just a snooze
Yet we fail to heed the open clues
That surround us for our good
That what goes for the goose, goes for the gander
For God has an inviolable agenda

And the rules of engagement always the same
For the female and the male
The poor and the rich
The ugly and the chic
The giant and the dwarf
The quickest and the sloth
The sharpest and the dullest
The black and the white

You and they God meant to fly
You and they He meant to rise
You and they He meant to climb the mountains
And rise to the top giving thanks for the Fountain
You and they to win the game
Cause you and they are of the same race—
The human race
Running the same survival race

Black, white, red or yellow,
All came here the same mysterious way
And all will leave the same mysterious way!......
Yet we constitutionalise our misconceptions
Of life to our misled congregations
Indoctrinate them with bigoted notions
That send them panting with joy
Or jumping off the bandwagon

With ambition swelling their chests
To carve out other roads to trek
But still fail to make the grade
In the likeness of God's Image scale

We formulate long formal protocols
To cover up our many moral downfalls
Brew grief in the stomach of the oppressed
Swollen with swallowed bricks of suppression

Seek vengeance when we are hurt
Rather than forgive all with love
Letting our tempers run amok
When we are meant to be rocks
Our leaders send us to wars
To settle fake diplomatic scores
In place of the advocacy of peace on earth
And good will to all men

These loveless drills with pungent innuendoes
Compel the eruption of our dormant volcanoes
To spew out the umbilical pulse of change
That sanity may finally restore constraints
So we may once more truly Love all
Singeing all hate with the lava of love
Drowning all hate with peace and joy
As true likenesses of the Images of God

Twins Of Fate

We are all alike, like it or not!
Do we not all want to be the first
To break the record in any test
That displays our good Homo sapiens traits
Do we not all want to be the best
In any field of human endeavour
That offers mankind the chance to savour
The abundant flavours of Gods favours

Through the talents that we favour
In science and technology
Invention or agronomy
In art or astrology
In any activity that facilitates
The development of the human race
Do we not all want to be the greatest
Nor indeed want to be celebrated

For deeds of unrivalled excellence
In humanity's quest for progress
Do we not want to be the best of the best
In the field of comedy say
Do we not want to be the funniest
Giving therapeutic brakes to all
From the stress of toxic anxiety
Of living in our modern societies

Do we not want to be the most favoured
In mankind's choice of heroes
Do we not want to be the most loved
In return for our Living our lives with Love
Do we not want to be the most appreciated
In return for others appreciated
The most faithful
For our commitment to our duties to God and man

The most remembered and adored
For our selfless services to our fellow men
Do we not want to be the best in everything
As participants in the adventure of existence
Are we not gifted novices in the diverse crafts of life
With burning desires to scale the heights
As the geniuses we are meant to be
Which when thwarted or jailed in prejudice

Conspires against the adventurer
Driving him to raise the flag of rebellion
Trapping his dreams in a cold asylum
Dragging him down the street of disillusion
To loose commitment to reality
To humanity and society
To sincerity and loyalty
To civility and cordiality

To integrity and morality
To non-commitment to serving humanity
Non commitment to decency and decorum
To kindness and compassion

To truth and honesty
To transparency and clemency
Non commitment to the pursuance of peace
Non-commitment to the society

Non-commitment even to himself
But commitment to desperation and destruction
Playing into the jaws of rejection or incarceration
Or cowering to the ill-bred bullies
Who demand the most from the tills
Of those less privileged than them
Less elevated in status than them
Less supported in numbers than them

Disadvantaged by race
Demoralised by hatred
Carving and shaping the boomerangs
With their selfies on their blades
Magnifying the marks we make
On the sands of time without end
With haunting scenes of suicides and fratricides
Homicides, matricides and recurring genocides

Creating a disgruntled and disfranchised mankind
Creating a fake humanity in the style
Of disembodied demigods
Cocooned in a bastard, insensitive time capsule
Facing the future it did not foresee
Because it closed its eyes to all the signs
That point the arrows
To the regenerative paths of Love!

The Selective Game

Security gadgets scanning the world
Cannot stem the hair-raising hacking
Nor the boom, pow, banging
Reverberating all around the planet
Showcasing the prices we have to pay
For replacing Justice for all with justice for some
Freedom for all with freedom for some
Opportunities for all with opportunities for some

Success for all with success for some
Kindness to all with kindness to some
Happiness for all with happiness for some
Security for all with security for some
Wealth for all with wealth for some
Good health for all with good health for some
Good education for all
With good education for some

Good social services for all
With just for some
Peace for all with peace for some
We replaced praise for all with disgrace for some
Unity for all with disunity for some
Brotherliness with enmity with some
Sympathy for all with apathy for some
Compassion for all with insensitivity for some

Bringing some down
Raising some up
Rather than helping all to rise
Sharing God's gifts with all
Rather than cutting some others out
Mentoring some people
But discouraging some others
Generosity only to some rather than all

Stepping on each other to rise to the top
Rather than raising each other up to the top
As likenesses of the Image of God
Treating some with brutality
Rather than all with kindness
Promoting self-centred agendas
Image promoting agendas
Power promoting agendas

Hate promoting agendas
Self aggrandising agendas
All forms of divisive agendas
Rather than all-inclusive agendas
Based on the principles of universal Love
For the good of all humanity
As those who are made
In the likenesses of the Image of God

The Fermentation

Wherever we look there is despair
Where there should have been hope
Wherever we go there is fear in the air
Where there should have been joy
Wherever we look there is despondency
Where there should have been confidence
Rather than passivity by the deprived
Whose hands are tied by our loveless systems

Fear staring at the old and the young
Treading gingerly on the paths of the juggernauts
With blasts of infamous offers of largess
Drowning all reasons
Trading glamour for humour
Waywardness for progress
Shamelessness for style
Debauchery for freedom

Flagging the illusion of liberation
Wedded with unparalleled confusion
In the mirage of modern life by
Modern man and modern woman
Modern boy and modern girl
Modern terms and modern facts
That negate all the beneficial functions
Of Living Love in human interactions

In our total amnesia
Of who we really are
And what we are expected to do
As the likenesses of the Image of God
We no more distinguish between right and wrong
Anything goes has scrambled our world
Parents and children are forced
To defame and degrade others

Rather than support each other
To intimidate rather than encourage each other
To coerce others to the addictive negation of truth
Encouraging the practice of 'alternative truths'
Abbreviated truths
Qualified truths
Hybridised truths
Legalised truths

Castrated truths
Specialised truths
Imaginary truths
Anything but The Truth
The cardinal attribute of those
Created in the likenesses of the Image of God
Who should not falsify facts no matter what
Or do anything self-effacing and abhorrent

To the nature and sanctity of God
Yet we do not frown at outrageous ploys
To get what we want
Like the puppets on the bill-boards of fame

There is no more indecency in complicity
Nor guilt in our exhibition of hypocrisy
Even at the altar of confession
Even before the hangman's noose

Even at the foot of the cross on the hill
Even with the consuming fire of hell on our heels
We defiantly hold our grounds
When pressured for accounts
When our survival in the game is paramount
We look for means of escape
Blaming others for our mistakes
Implicating them in our missteps

Degrading our likenesses of the Image of God
Our leaders throw sand in our soup
Pepper in our eyes
Dirt in our milk with witty faked smiles
Making us give in to the ploys
That make it difficult for us to achieve
What we were meant to achieve
Or do what we were given to do

For all mankind's good
As likenesses of the Image of God
With the ennobling upright expressions
Of His Love in our operations
In all areas of human aspirations
Shattering our beliefs in our selves
Turning our world into a battle ground
Of bedazzled antelopes trampling each other down

In the collective amnesia
Castigating and humiliating each other
Plotting and degrading each other
Railing over this, that and the other
Crowding our days with crucibles of doom
Painting black white
Or the other way around for a prize
Spouting deceptive wry smiles

And grinding our teeth
When our plans are breached
Rejecting the credence of maintained honesty
And embracing brazen abrogations
Of time tested and sanitised traditions
Cynicism is now the escape
Of the dejected populace
The bamboozled gullible hungry flocks

The Disintegration

Bamboozled in politics and religion
Fashion trends and food fads
Truly, we have lost the grip
To the why and wherefore
All humans breathe the air
As beneficiaries of the nature we have betrayed
We have lost the grip
To the why and wherefore

We are made in the likeness
Of the Image of God
We have lost the grip
To the fact that the Lord our God is Love
And does nothing outside His Love
And as His images so should we
We have lost the grip
To the why and wherefore that Love is in us

If not that we may validate each other
As He validates us
Giving to each other
As He gives us
Forgiving each other
As He forgives us
Pollinating each other
Like the bees and birds do flowers

That we may bloom and yield in plenty
Spreading beauty in variegated hues
In fulfillments of nature's goals
Not dismembering God's cardinal rules
HELPING being the cardinal word
The magic rod that conjured up
All that exists to aid all mankind
In our eternal developmental quests

The generative act that we must undertake
To make all talents manifest
At home or in the fields
In the factories and offices
Wherever humans operates
To make our world a better place
Where all creatures coexist with nothing but Love
Unconditional and helping Love

The creative word is 'HELP'
The friendly word is Help
The generous word is Help
The nurturing word is Help
The just word is Help
The humane word is Help
But we deny help where it is needed most
Drown its tender song with indifferent notes

We drive over gaping holes in the ground
Where others crawl
Expecting them to jump with their feet in bonds
To play Hercules without the horn

Stride blindfolded through the storms
Skip to the sky and jump over the moon
By the skin of their teeth
Trapping them in a perpetual battle field

We do not evenly share
The icing on the national cake
We stab each other in the back
And justify our acts as tit for tat
In the collective amnesia
Of the Love we should share
Through kindness and forgiveness
As the likenesses of the Image of God

We push others to the back,
Our heads tilted with bloated pride
Or lick the boss's swollen boots
And grease the boss's sweaty hands too
Accepting the unacceptable
Doing the unimaginable
Stooping to our lowest conceivable
To gain any amount of grounds

With those who wear the crown
And sit on thrones with royal frowns
We turn blind eyes to vices to climb the ladders
We cut corners at the expense of others
We spread thorns on others paths
But cover ours with fragrant flowers
It is me, me, me and mine
I must have the best from the mines

The best car
With golden bars
The best houses
The best clothes
The best suits
The best shoes
The best purses
The best horses

The best taste for anything
Women, men, friends and mates
Jobs, marriages and of course sex
The best of life with all it takes
The best of everything
In short, the best the world can offer
Without a thought for the other
Forgetting the virtue of selflessness

As true likenesses of the Image of God
We often sabotage our own dreams
But blame the other for our misdeeds
With jealousy striking harder than the hammer
Igniting crippling fevers of wounded pride
Forging yet other deadly sins
Unfitting for the likenesses of the Image of God
Who should always be on our guards

At functions we familiarly gloat
Our eyes wide and afloat
Roaming from side to side
With cunning and studied style

We feverishly grab the goods
Like spoilt children who snatch the goodies
At Birthday and Christmas parties
Humiliating our likenesses

Of the Image of God
At the circuses of merry imposters
We raise our glasses with mixed sentiments
And toast accomplices with indifference
Spreading conspirators' grins
On faces flushed with jin
Mocking our likenesses of the Image of God
In our callousness and depravity

Sometimes we adopt the look of regret
So we may seem blessed
Yet as Judas Iscariot did
We betray humanity with avarice
Supplemented with embedded calumny
Orchestrated in egomaniacal conspiracy
Engineered by the pharisaical rich
In our political theatres and cliques

We humiliate the other with our looks
We subjugate the other to servitude
Binding him in a straight jacket
Volunteered by the cronies in our pockets
All against our true nature
As likenesses of the Image of God
Who should give to Peter what we give to Paul
In justice and Love

We do not find it offensive to grind our teeth
In the face of the meek
Because we are above their means
And pay the piper when we please
We pander to the wolves
Or play to the galleries
Of our brain washed auxiliaries
All against our true nature

As the likenesses of the Image of God
We gag the young with flamboyant stunts
Strip weak minds of compassion
Treating victims without emotions
Standing by the strong against the weak
The lions against the ignorant sheep
Against our true nature
As likenesses of the Image of God

*F*ire *In* The Barn

We gravitate towards that which scintillates
That which captivates
That which excites
That which is hype
Exotic
Euphoric
Emblematic
Trendy

All against the nature of the endowed exponents
Of the rationality and benevolence of God
Who were meant to leap after we have looked
To stand up for what is good
To aspire to only do what is good
Motivated by the good others do
Uplifted by the wisdom of mentors
Supported and encouraged by heroes

And nurtured with hands of fellowship
For all mankind's benefit
We were meant to gain strength in friendship
Not spend good times in gossips
In spite of that girls gossip
Boys gossip
Men gossip
Women gossip

The old gossip
The young gossip
Maligning each other
Ridiculing each other
Degrading each other
Demeaning each other
Defaming each other
Demonising each other

Dehumanising each other
Destroying each other
Passing the dark art from one to the other
The young learning from the old
Perpetuating the alienating throes
As the young copy us cheating
The young copy us stealing
The young copy us lying

The young copy us swearing
The young copy us sneering
They copy us doing all the things
We are not supposed to do
They copy our moral laxity
They copy our depravity
Our lack of respect for one another
Inability to stand unyielding to infamy

They copy our inconsistencies
They repeat our prejudices
Our hypocrisy
Our bigotry

Our frivolity
Our insincerity
They copy every step we take
They have no choice but to replicate

The things we do in the same trail
And cannot help but fall where we fell
Trip where we tripped
Drown in the cesspool of our mistakes
Or soar to the skies by chance or fate
Life for them is in constant litigation
Life for them is in constant gravitation
From doubt to confusion

From rebellion to conformity
From saintliness to ignominy
Dangling on the jagged edge
Of what is right and what is wrong
Of what to do and not to do
They are the victims of our exploits
In the jungle politics of our distorted lives
Where the blind now leads the deaf

The greedy salivates for more preys
And hypocrites pose as saints
We bribe them with gifts
Just as we do dogs with treats
We make promises we cannot keep
Pulling wool over eyes of limping flocks of sheep
Confusing facts with fictions
Replacing truth with fabrications

Rendering it inconsequential
Making life a game of trivia
Can we justify these assaults
On humanity's vital forces
In the constant tug of wars
Between Deceit and Honesty
Can we justify this tug of war
Between Cruelty and Kindnesses

Can we justify this tug of war
Between Vanity and Humility
Can we justify this tug of war
Between Selfishness and Generosity
Can we justify this tug of war
Between Injustice and Justice
Can we justify this tug of war
Between War and Peace

Can we justify this tug of war
Between Good and Evil
Can we justify this tug of war
Between Hatred and Love
Can we justify this tug of war
Between Enmity and Friendliness
Can we justify this tug of war
Between Sadness and Happiness

Can we really justify this tug of war
Between Taking and Giving
Can we really justify
Humiliation rather than Adoration

Can we really justify
Suppression rather Liberation
Can we really justify
Judgment rather than Encouragement

Can we really justify
Hindering rather than Empowering
Can we really justify
Vindictiveness rather than Magnanimity
Can we really justify
Maliciousness rather than Benevolence
Can we really justify
Disgrace rather than Praise

Can we really justify
Revenge rather than Forgiveness
Can we really justify
Degradation rather than Honour
Can we really justify
Oppression rather Liberation
Can we really justify
Insincerity rather than sincerity

Can we really justify
Lies rather than truth and reality
Banning empathy from the shores of emotions
Reducing humanity to a band of robots
Strutting the earth in human forms
Demonising the innocent, adulating the guilty
Denouncing humanity in every community
Failing to see the smoking fire in the barn

The Perversion

Boomerangs do come home
Having taken life from oak beams from our homes
Their bodies covered with ballads
Painted with hues from our family pallets
Symbolising our hopes and dreams
Clouding our visions with choking fumes
Spewed out from the home stews
That characterise our family brews

The child waxing strong in the brand
Cannot fail to brand the boomerang
With tattoos from the family air loom
Inciting him to lie and bully at school
Or fight and cheat a handful
In the law of like father like his brood
Do all the things the parents do
With no regrets but much conceit

Nature setting up a protective screen
Giving him time to stand on his feet
At puberty he investigates and speculates
Sampling the fruits from the cabinet
Of the parental tutelage
Peer pressure in constant collusion
With increasing delusion compel attention
The youngster capitulates with burning intention

To one or the other in equal proportion
Forging more boomerangs
In the fire of mixed emotions
Concretised with aspirations and the volitions
To conquer the foes of his pet desires
Still held prisoner with the shy demeanour
Of the uninitiated adventurer
Making his debut on the world stage

The teenager steps out to set the world on fire
With the tentacles of a starved octopus
And the will of an irruptive volcano
Spewing its characteristic lava
Ravaging the world with inconceivable caviars
Of compounded hot recipes
Declaring his pent-up emotions
Blazing the trail with passion and visions

In music and mission
In dance and fashion
In religion and invention
In ideology and philosophy
In leisure and pleasure
In relationship and partnership
In politics and friendship
In morality and individuality

In creativity and productivity
In materiality and spirituality
In coquetry and sexuality
In logic and ethics
The list is long and the implications quite scary
Painting the world with projections
Of apocalyptic images
That confuse and confound

The Acculturation

At colleges the broths of acculturation thicken
The scope of intellection broadens
Sororities and fraternities accentuate
Adulterate and obliterate
Duplicate and sublimate
Consecrating and sanctifying peculiar notions
Of what is right and what is not
Formulating outlandish ideologies

That typify their insecurity in the challenging world
Staggering with instability
Suppurating with insincerity
Hardened with insensitivity
Debased with hypocrisy
Unreliable with inconsistency
Intolerant with bigotry
Immoral with carnality and sensuality

Crippled by racism in all fields of life
Jaundiced with xenophobia and other phobias
Deformed by intolerance and other vices
Beleaguered by greed induced strife
In internal and international organisations
In foundations and institutions
In politics and religion
In sports and sundry exertions

The youth retorts in kind
So the blackmail boldly strides
Through the campus grooms and brides
Greed courting greed, phobia espousing phobias
Racism promoting racism
Discrimination sponsoring it's kith and kin
Bigotry lauding bigotry
Hypocrisy declaring its stance

In the law of like attracting likes
And the struggle continues without slack
The graduate then raises his war flag
The son replicating the father
The daughter replicating the mother
The initiate replicating the mentor
The novice the master
The blind leading the blinded

From one generation to the next
From one ancestor to the next.....
Then step by step the tie is broken
The youth embraces the storm head on
Armed with visions from the crib
Garnished with the boost from college
Or despair from slummy cottages
The youth becomes a man

The girl becomes a woman
The prospector becomes adventurous
Principles give way to expediency
Favours are sought

Favours are bought
Favours are demanded
Favours are given
Hands washing other dirty hands

Abandoning constraint with indignation
Morality with the deceit of freedom
Wallowing in the mud of modernism
With time tested edicts
Now on modern chopping boards
He joins the club of lost heroes
In the bungled fight for survival
To deface Love with the race or gender card

Besmear Love by incriminating others
Reject Love by killing others
Butcher Love by fabricating facts
Defame Love by disgracing others
Demean Love by conspiring against others
This time flag bearer like any other
Blasts down life's road in merry weather
Moulding impressions of himself
Casting shadows of himself

On the walls of time
For others standing in line
The pose he takes is either quack or quaint
His steps fraught with concern
From season to season
The cosmic brew is seasoned
With the emissions of his volitions

On boomerangs forged with pent emotions
With messages carved in wild confusion
Which return in course with precision
From hour to hour from minute to minute
The struggling novice juggles the jumbled rings
Displaying his acquired survival tricks
He chooses to lie like his father
To pretend like his preacher

To pontificate like his professor
To insult like his sister
Who nags like her mother
To intimidate like his boss
To insinuate like his abuser
To implicate like his opponent
To subjugate like a bully
To cheat like his rival

To bribe like politicians or his colleagues
To defame like his neighbour
To dehumanise like a racist
The boomerang hence perpetually launched
For us to catch in a perpetual chain
As son becomes the father
The daughter becomes the mother
The student becomes the master

The young becomes the old
And streams of eloquent epitaphs
Haunt the graves of the savaged pasts
And the youth struggles between reason and wit

The voice of prudence questioning his skills
As patriotism and nationalism collide in mid air
Precipitating bigotry and hostility with fan fare
Assaulting and captivating the young initiate

Tickling his navigational antennas
Driving him into the cesspool of deviants
Of political and ideological gurus
Populating the adventurous world of possibilities
He succumbs to flattery or bribery
Intimidation and confrontations
The stimulations of drugs and debauchery
Lured by vanity and rivalries

The plot thickens
His heart hardens
His paths beclouded
By the fouled emissions
From his contaminated volitions
His views now uncertain
His steps precarious
His world distorted and dangerous!

More Destabilising Factors

Through the elementary, middle and high schools,
Universities of the establishment or of the hoods
Our intentions keep shaping the boomerangs
Our volitions firing the loaded weapons
Of conflicting bags of tricks
Which drown our hopes of relief
From the long list of our griefs
As everyone schemes for riches

Stoking the fever of greed
Insurance companies duping their clients
Doctors panting for appointments
Saving time not so much their patients
Politicians bamboozling the electorate
Forcing their wills over those of the populace
Manufacturers and retailers preying on consumers
Farmers and gardeners growing GMOs

Performers and entertainers perverting reality
Priests and historians confusing facts
Dancers and sportsmen drilling the nerves
Mailmen and firemen bearing much strain
Caterers and chefs burnishing the pallet
The gurus and spiritualists drifting in fantasies
Physically or whimsically misleading the novices
Literarily or orally, singing the same hymn

The introvert or extrovert both out of rhythm
The recluse or the showboat looking out for self
The successful or unsuccessful fainting with stress
The loud mouthed and fowl mouthed jarring nerves
The young and the old clamouring for gold
The vain stepping on everyone's toes.
The egocentric boasting
The violent blustering

The selfish hoarding
The tall looking down his high horse
Pride in tow with kinky social mores
The short blazing the Napoleonic trail
The dwarf fighting with self esteem
The slow dragging his feet
The fast overshooting the mark
The handsome often vain

The rich getting greedier
The poor, subservient
The good looking, presumptuous
The plain, vulnerable
The smart, over ambitious
The dim witted, used
The white, prejudiced and divisive
The black the same and defensive

The student starving for true knowledge
The teacher starving
The novice compromised
The master egocentric

The citizen fighting to retain his rights
The foreigner begging for some rights
The refugee and alien without any rights
All setting the boomerangs on their chartered courses

The happy keeping his fingers crossed
The sad backing away from all the fuss
The sane calculating and plotting
The insane being unaware of his fate
The depressed blaming all but self
The suppressed struggling to exhale
The mature walking with jaunty steps
The other, blundering with confused gaits

Governors and mayors winning electoral jackpots
Aldermen and senators feathering their nests
Judges and janitors mortgaging human fates
Policemen enforcing self-made laws
Soldiers killing for national greed and power
Lawyers lying with legal jargons
Clerks keeping doctored books
Magicians deceiving with sleights of hands

Sometimes dabbling with the occult
Inventors pushing the limitless limit
Investors cashing in on their gimmicks
Bankers turning into biblical whales
Money lenders into devouring sharks
Fashion designers exploiting ingrained perversions
Breaking bond with decorum and grace
Gymnasts stretching limbs to breaking points

Sports-men going any length to win
Craftsmen cheating when demands increase
Singers parading their gifts to impress
Artists painting humanity's fate
Newscasters and broadcasters stretching facts
Beauticians mocking nature with plastics and paints
Physicians and specialists making claims
Playwrights satirising and fantasising life

Directors painting quixotic scenes of life
Actors giving themselves for parts
Managers intimidating subordinates
Producers trading with others gifts
Employing their expertise to achieve their goals
Most times ignoring the Living Love approach
Store owners inflating the price of goods
No matter where and how produced

Dressing their goods with fancy tricks
Tailored for ensnaring the spendthrifts
Floor managers catching roving eyes
Luring them into tempting isles
Employees losing even lives
In the bid of making ends meet
And keeping some roofs over their heads
Farmers adulterating their seeds

To get fake bombastic yields
Farm managers exploiting the workers
Distributors circumventing tariffs
Retailers quadrupling their profits

Realtors gathering where they did not sow
Homeowners drowning their lives with bills
Insurance companies exploiting our fears
Bankers in collusion giving them hand shakes

Politicians masquerading as nation builders
Religious leaders exploiting seekers
Homemakers struggling with many odds
To keep their families in tight bond
Home wreckers disbanding family bands
All scripted on our returning boomerangs
Igniting sparks of contention and revolution
In the minds of all generations

In addition to the strangle hold
Of these perversions that have left us cold
And crippled humanity young and old
Plunging us headlong on the path
Of a frightening karmic avalanche
We are left to dig ourselves out
Of the self-inflicted repercussions
In the regurgitated and vile imitation

Of the child cursing because the parents did
The youth stealing because his mate did
His mate stealing because his parents did
The family discriminating because their neighbours did
Companies cheating because their financiers did
Their financiers doing because the establishment does
The establishment doing because it exists
In the self-promoting reality of capitalism

Racism, socialism or communism
Now we are being irresistibly drawn
Through the eye of nemesis's needle
What we have sown we must now reap
For quilting infamy and decay on the tapestry of life
Defying the Creators laws
Carving out our own perverting ways

Damning our lives in every way
Dreamers hang their hopes on fate
Achievers catching the birds in their nest
Path blazers and hair raisers the same
Health givers try to maintain life
Caterers restoring the fuel of life
Air pilots and crews defying gravity
Pickers and baggers suffering for pittance
Writers looking for truth pushing pens

Jewellers mimicking beauty with germs
Sculptors mimicking nature in daring style
Composers giving vent to their moods
Conductors interpreting them at their whims
Trumpeters and flutists mimicking emotions
Violinists and saxophonists expressing emotions
Drummers and cellists, guitarist and pianists,
Bassist, bassoonist, hornists and vocalist

Vying for fame in celebrated pavilions
All playing their own conceived versions
Of the symphony of Life
Barely caring whether or not
They abide by the laws of nature
That are woven into the laws of Love
Binding us willy-nilly to the Will of God
Who made us in the likeness of His own Image

Food For Thought

For how long should we let these go on
In place of Love for all
As likenesses of the Image of God
For how long should we let hypocrisy go on
In place of probity
As likenesses of the Image God
For how long should we let bigotry go on
In place of tolerance

As likenesses of the Image of God
For how long should we let racism go on
In place of building a happy family of races
As willed by God in His Law of Love
For how long should we let all the phobias go on
Xenophobia, homophobia, this and the other phobia
The megalomania and all the other manias
In a world that functions only with unbiased power of Love

Do we hate ourselves
Do we fear ourselves
Do we accuse ourselves
Why do we not ignore ourselves
Why do we not demean ourselves
Why do we not incriminate ourselves
Detest ourselves
Discriminate against ourselves

Blatantly lie against ourselves
Reject ourselves
Suspect ourselves
Criticise ourselves
Malign ourselves
Obstruct ourselves
Deny ourselves
Cheat ourselves

Why do we not deceive ourselves
Belittle ourselves
Undermine ourselves
Betray ourselves
Deride ourselves
Suppress ourselves
Oppress ourselves
Conspire against ourselves

Why do we not inhibit ourselves
Why do we not implicate ourselves
Why do we not retaliate against ourselves
Why do we not denounce ourselves
Why do we not Dispossess ourselves
Discredit ourselves
Dishonour ourselves
Dislike ourselves

Disrespect ourselves
Deprive ourselves
Destroy ourselves
Demonise our selves

Dehumanise ourselves
Why do we not look down on ourselves
Why not disapprove of ourselves
Why not incite ourselves

Why not intimidate ourselves
Why not disregard ourselves
Why not mislead ourselves
Why not criticise ourselves
Why then do all these to others
We claim human nature is at play
Would what is good for the goose
Not be good for the gander in that case

From morning till night we guard our trails
Monopoly is our favourite game
We are sharks in car parks
Even on benches in the parks
In busses and trains too the sick may stand
We cater to self in all the land
At all times without regret
With our hearts bleeding of love bereft

The Guilt

With the lingering vestiges of virtuous living
Relegated to irrelevance and ignominy
Aided by prancing sycophants as confidants
Everywhere we look
Looms the frowning face of decency
The lost look of despondency
The grinding teeth of patience
The wringing hands of tolerance

The rolling eyes of disbelief
The frowning faces of discontent
The tearful eyes of regret
The sad looks of rejection
The dreamy looks of the lost
The yearning looks of hope
The haunting looks of disparity
The baneful looks of despair

The shy looks of insecurity weaken us
The lost looks of abandonment discredit us
The hungry looks for relief and peace ask why
The sad looks of the oppressed catch our breath
The yearning looks for Love sadden us
Along with the sneering looks of bigotry
The taunting looks of hate disarm us
The defying looks of power frighten us

The devouring looks of greed accuse us
The sensual looks of lust disturb us
The angry looks of disdain incite us
The piercing looks of antagonism scare us
The list is long and the implications ominous
These legacies of perversions and recriminations
Now confront mankind everywhere
Brimming with overarching passion for change

The Undeniably Truth

As we speak the looming reality
Is that all lives are in jeopardy
The world around is up in arms
Fighting the terror of arms with arms
The law of reciprocity always in operation
The claims and counter claims of aggressions
Doubling their strength in lightening successions
Suppression succeeding discriminations

Bigotry succeeding exclusion
Deprivation succeeding prejudice,
Injustice succeeding intolerance,
Greed succeeding monopoly,
Dehumanisation succeeding defamation
Hatred succeeding segregation
Power mongering succeeding egocentricity
Racism succeeding separatism

Defacing the awesome canvas
Of God's artistic masterpieces
For if all the trees were the oak
If all the palms were coconut palms
If all the bushes were nettles
If all the grass were elephant grass
If all the animals were lions
If all the fishes were sharks

If all the insects were mosquitoes,
If all the reptiles were cobras
If all the seasons were winter
If all the lands were deserts
If all the fruits were banana
If all the meals were fish and chips
If all musical instruments have only one note
And all the climates were the same

If all the meat was beef
If all the drinks were Jin
If all the songs were raps
And all the music were classical
If all humans were males
If all humans were females
And if all humans looked the same
Dressed the same way

Spoke the same way
And ate the same food everyday
What a strange world that would be
Then why scheme against racial diversity
Which validates racial equality
And justifies social equity
Exercising the feeling of empathy
Preventing the perpetration of the hatred

Of one man and another
Cause nobody wants to be hated
Nor his or her life degraded
And as the likenesses of the Image of God

Should we not do unto others
As we would want done to us
We don't want to be devalued
Then why do you devalue others

Is that doing to those others
As we would want done to us
As the likenesses of the Image of God
We don't like to be cheated
Then why do we cheat others
Is that doing to those others
As we would like done to us
As the likenesses of the Image of God

We don't like to be ill treated
Then why do we ill-treat others
Is that doing to those others
As we would like done to us
We don't like to be maligned
Then why do we malign others
Is that doing to those others as
As we would like done to us

We don't like to be marginalised
Then why do we marginalise others
Is that doing to those others
As we would like done to us
We don't want to be rejected
Then why do so to others
Is that doing to those other
As we would want done to us

We don't want to be stereotyped
Then why do so to others
Is that doing to those others
As we would want done to us
We don't like to be incriminated
Why do so to others
Is that doing to those others
As we want done to us

We don't like to be falsely accused
Why do so to others
Is that doing to them
As we want done to us
In the law of give and take
Of those made in the Likeness
Of the Image of God
With His all-embracing Love

We don't like to be racially profiled
Why do so to others
Is that doing to them
The way you want done to you
We don't like to be ridiculed
Why do so to others
Is that doing to them
The way you would want done to you

We don't like to be dispossessed
Why do so to others
Have we done to them
As we would want done to us

We don't like to be enslaved
Why do so to others
Have we done to them
The way we would want done to us

You don't like to be demonised
Why do so to others
Have you done to them
The way you want done to you
You don't want to be a pawn
Why make others pawns
Have you done to them
The way you would want done to you

In the law of give and take
In the law of Love your neighbour
As you truly love yourself
In the law of reciprocity
In all the laws of Love
Of those made in the likeness
Of the Image of God
With His creative energy of Love

You don't want to be abused We
don't want to be accused We
don't want to be suppressed We
don't want to be oppressed We
do not want to be scammed Nor
bury our heads in the sand
When danger is at hand
We don't want to be ignored

You don't want to be debased
You don't want to be defaced
You do no want to be taunted
You do not want to be bullied
You don't want to be deceived
You don't want to be discriminated against
You don't want to be killed
You don't want to be deprived

We don't want to be vilified
We don't want to be condemned
We don't want to be abandoned
We don't want to be slighted Nor
do we want to be derided We
don't want our dreams stifled
Nor our efforts sabotaged
We only want to succeed in life

And so do others of all the tribes

The Reaping

Our dreams from the womb
Become lost in the hoods and saloons
Our consciences mortgaged at the breath
Of contaminated air in the survival fair
Choking our birthrights leaving us marooned
In the social and political desert sand-dunes
Our oaths of allegiance to fruitful lives doomed
And our boomerangs come spinning in the induced gale

Gathering more choking dusts on their blades
For the young and the old
The weak and the bold
The rich and poor
The smart and not
The White and not
The Black and not
The Good looking and not

The Out going or not
The Retired or not
The Talented or not
The Married or not
The Divorced or not
The Tall or not
For the Fat or not
For the Short or not

The Happy or not
The Starving or not
The Blind or not
The Handicapped or not
The Deprived or not
The Rejected or not
The Incarcerated or not
The Educated or not

The Beautiful or not
The Handsome or not
The Strong or not
The Loved or not
The Employed or not
The Happy or not
The Accomplished or not
The Prince or Princess

The King or Queen
The Pope or Cardinal
The priest or priestess
The monk or nun
The Christian or Muslim
The Hindu or Buddhist
The agnostic or atheist
The gay or lesbian

The hypocrite or bigot
The ruler or the ruled
The mother or the father
The son or the daughter

The brother or the sister
The villagers or the city dwellers
The urbanites or the cosmopolitans
The citizens or the immigrants

The boomerangs are gathering strength
In countries and continents
Highlands and lowlands
In wetlands and dry lands
In caves and mountains
In jungles and deserts
In the air and on land
In huts and mansions

In resorts and prisons
On the streets and the beaches
At home and retreats
At work and at play
Night and day
Unswerving from their well-marked tracks
We have nowhere now to hide
We have to face the rolling tides

Through our leaders who are our totem poles
The emblems of our thwarted goals
Set on golden calves of ambition
The agents of the dreams
Of all who surf on stormy seas
That sweep the shores of jumbled creeds
With the waves of divide and conquer
Crashing and drowning pledges made with honour

Changing say a nation under God
Into a nation in a choking fog
With changeling dragons on the prowl
Guarding broods of wandering pilgrims
In quest of the grail of fame and gain
Our greed make the dragons drool
Our malice grow the dragons claws
Our hatred fan the dragons flames

Our deceits sculpt their scaly tough hides
Our lies stretch the dragons tongues
Our jealousies give heat to their breaths
Our insensitivity make their skins thick
And the dragons lash with tripled skill
Simply put, the leaders we choose
Are perfect clones of our imperfections
And embodiments of our transgressions

Poised for us to see ourselves
Posed for us to judge ourselves
What they lack ring our bells
What they say echo from our wishing wells
What they do are what we have bred
What they think run riot in our heads
What they don't do
We have left out too

Causes And Effects

Living in a world of cause and effect
The wound hurts
Because the skin is torn
The dog's tail wags
Because the dog is happy
But tucked between the legs
Because the dog is hurt
Or may be guilty of one prank or another

Heads of states anywhere on earth
Are what they are because we have them made
The well sculpted totem poles
That vicariously carry our every mole
The whirling Boomerangs that bear
The irksome traits we share
They amplify the hate we hide
They transmit the bigotry we hide

They magnify the indignity we hide
Symbolise the hypocrisy we hide
Dramatise the biases we hide
Exaggerate the phobias we hide
Exploit the prejudices we hide
Demonstrate the greed we hide
Capitalise on the gluttony we hide
Emphasise the felonies we commit

Illustrate all of our intransigences
In the school teachers who bully
The farmers who adulterate their produce
The manufacturers who fake products
Law enforcers who break the law
Writers who plagiarise
Athletes who take performance drugs
All fly their phantom flags

Boxers who fake their punches
Fly their phantom flags
So do the wrestlers who fake their falls
Students who cheat in exams
Pedophiles who deny their addictions
Rapists who blame their victims
Parents who neglect their children
All fly their phantom flags

Attorneys who falsify facts
Fly their phantom flags
People who bribe
Fly their phantom flags
People who scam
Fly their phantom flags
The ones who rob others
Fly their phantom flags

The deviants who defraud
People who fake their identities
People who conspire against others
People who destroy others' lives

People who commit adultery
People who are jealous or envious
Aggressive or pugilistic
Fly their phantom flags

All who are insensitive
All who are acquisitive
All who are contentious
All who are pretentious
All who are brash or crude
All who are egotistic
Who care less for the underdogs
All fly our leaders phantom flags

Those who intimidate others
Those who deceive others
Ones who castigate others
Ones who demoralise others
Who conspire or destroy others' lives
All vicariously launched the twirling boomerangs
That now return with resounding bangs
Cause Likes have attracted their irrefutable likes

For the boomerang always returns
To where it was spun
What went around has come around
For all the leaders of our world
Are clones of our own flesh and blood
Seeds of our wombs
To hold and to groom
No matter the wounds

Masqueraders

It takes a village to raise a child
It takes a society masquerading progress
To sabotage the maintenance
Of human dignity and integrity
Sucking the blood of resistance to infamy
Breaking the back of conformity to excellence
And commitment to morality and propriety
Perverting all time-tested realities

In the collective amnesia
Of our sacred duties as likenesses
Of the Image of God
Masquerading progress progressively perverts
Even the household pets
Let alone mankind's all-time quest
For sane displays of Love among men
As likenesses of the Image of God

In the enforcement of the laws
The guardianship of jurisprudence
In the preservation of life
The prevention of strife
In the protection of the innocent
The observation of civil rights
Human rights and freedom of Life
And the maintenance of the rule of equity

Masquerading blind progress
Has distorted our spiritual perceptions
Broken the back of excellence
In our pursuance of personal goals
Like a harlot, the permissive troll
In callous abandonment and levity
Has opened doors for shifty eyed brigands
To soiree with system bred charlatans

Neglecting victims of civic neglect
In the collective amnesia
Of the virtue of compassion
As likenesses of the Image of God
Who should always endeavour
To care for all with Love
Permissiveness has connived at greed
And glorified underhanded deals

Joked at prevailing vices
Blinked at gravitation to vile obsessions
Encouraged money fetching addictions
Brewed laxity and infatuations
Foiling the purpose of our being made
In the likeness of the Image of God
In the perverted illusion of progress
We have turned away from all constraint

Generating the effusive atmosphere of euphoria
The pervading notions of invincibility and infallibility
Are peacock feathers on our top hats
Our exhibition of brashness and insensitivity

Luxuriate in the violation of ethical norms
In all human pursuits no matter the odds
All against the true nature of those made
In the likeness of the Image of God

In entertainments anything really goes
Opening the gate to unlimited scopes
Of hair and brow raising moral throes
In the collective amnesia and overthrow
Of decency and moral integrity
As likenesses of the Image of God
Their unfitting decadent plots
Sold on the silver screens round the globe

Digitised and propagated on videos
Vivified on gilded stages in cities and groves
Promoted in digs and mansions
For money and fame with all the passion
In the collective amnesia and overthrow
Of decency and moral integrity
Unfitting for the likenesses of the Image of God
Who should espouse all upright norms

Fashion designers strip women of shame
Placing mankind on the ware-ward lane
Paving the way for deviant adventurers
To justify these unnatural departures
The system fallen prey to manipulators
To bigots sharpening their weapons
Of suppression and oppression
Subverting the power of Love in Creation

Substituting the power of hatred
That grew from our unbridled pride
The power of greed
That grew from our self-indulgent needs
The power of wealth
That captivates and enslaves
The power of apathy
That has rendered mankind blind

Blind to the repercussions that plague us
In everything that has manifested
As fruits of our hands
Fruits of our words
Fruits of our wills
Against the will of God
For what we sow we must for ever reap
All nature bear witness for us to see

Ensued Chaos

The greedy has become the economist
The racist has become the nationalist
The flirt has become the gallant
The hypocrite has become the preacher
The bigot has become the purveyor of truth
The callous has become the prude
The murderer has become the hero
The ignoble has become the noble

The anarchist, the patriot
Up, down and down up
Lying has become alternative truth
Bribery, a mere gift we approve
Corruption has become a way of life!
A way to beat the perpetual strife
With ease born out of vice
The champion of perverted Love

All aspects of our lives are thus corrupted
And have veered away from the expectations
Of life styles of those who are made
In the likeness of the Image of God
From the food we eat
To the air we breath
From the way we speak
To the ways we breed

From the things we drink
To the ways we dress
The ways we relate have much at stake
The land is raped for commercial orgasms
Endangering both man and animal on it
In this humanity's assault on itself
Chaos reigns in every home
In every town around the globe

No man nor woman can really declare
That he or she has nothing to say
About all these spiritual frays
That have made our morality frail
Casting us into grotesque moulds
Milling around from coast to coast
Striking pretentious poses
As the likenesses of the Image of God

We intimidate and hurt one another
Lashing out as if possessed
Most unlike our Image of God
Threatening one another's very life
Making each feel totally insecure
Afraid for our lives everywhere
Insecure at the fair
Insecure in the air

Insecure in the farms
Insecure in our yards
Insecure in our churches
Our synagogues and mosques

Not sparing any day
Not safe at night
Even with the light
Unfitting life for the likenesses of the Image of God

Not safe in the village
Where there is much pillage
Not safe in the city
Where there is less pity
We are confronted with wrongs
And are haunted with guns
We are threatened with laws
And are threatened with wars

In a world without the Love of God
We are threatened by the elements
With the fall outs from our decadence
Catastrophic and devastating storms
Spilling out from nemesis's horn
The earth is shivering and quaking
Shaking off the slushy smelly scales
Of crusted effusions from the petrified glut

Of all humanity's bloated guts
In a world that is lacking in Living Love
And does not care for one another
But fear each other and suspect each other
Because we have failed to 'Love the other
As we Love ourselves'
And do to them as would be done to us
As should the likenesses of the Image of God

The counterfeited likeness of the Holy Image
Has been to our grave disadvantage
Has counterfeited all known human bids
To navigate through the labyrinths
Of the fake products of our ego driven ploys
Yielding its own corrupted versions of Love
Born from pride and adulterations
Lacking all spiritual foundation

Corruption

A. RELIGIOUS CORRUPTION

Our world is now totally corrupted
Our bonding acts of Love disrupted
Here, there and everywhere obstructed
What goes on here does so with the rest
For some it's more for some it's less
For some it is a matter of life and death
For some all the ways lead no where
For most complacency now reigns

All spheres of human life
Have suffered this corroding plight
And corruption has won the fight
Our politics is corrupted
Our social life is corrupted
Our social services are corrupted
Our gender identity is corrupted
The matrimonial institution is corrupted

The health care institution is corrupted
The agricultural system is corrupted
The food supply chain is corrupted
Our financial system is corrupted

Our employment system is corrupted
Our industrialists are corrupted
Our amusements are corrupted
Our religious systems are corrupted

Religious corruption sits on thrones
Consecrated with human souls
Wearing the inquisition crown
That bids us not to frown
At drilling confidence in faiths
That make humanity go astray
Throwing our yokes on Jesus,
Mohamed, Buddha and others

Making us act like clowns
Jesting round sacred grounds
Turning us into seasoned charlatans
Cavorting with marauding cankerworms
In circuses of spiritual banditry
Stamping out true self discovery
Of the irrefutable natural facts of life
Confusing spiritual and human rights

Doping our inquisitive minds
In overt religious camaraderie
With palliative pills of castles in heaven
Turning religion into a vending machine
For fast redemptive beverages
Religious corruption plays with humanity's survival
Opening doors to atheistic draughts
Which blow holes in the survival kit

With doctrinal presumptions
It dangles salvation for sale
For religious half-baked bags of cakes
It coins doctrines straight off the caps
Aggravating our spiritual handicaps
It breeds fanatics to execute its sour verdicts
From the Inquisitions to the Isis
From the Crusade, Al Qaeda and the Jihad

It makes true seekers become pawns
Brews complacent scapegoats and fawns
Turning committed converts into perverts
Feeding adherents with jaundiced verses
That make them lose all common sense
Christianity then fights Islamism
Buddhism contradicts Judaism
Each group claiming exclusive knowledge

About life here and after here
Cult priests, priestesses and rabbis
Cult mothers, fathers and bishops
Sect saints, imams and pastors
Become mere performers and actors
In the 'divine comedy' parody
That has confounded all humanity
Gurus, monks, all abound on the track

Degrading the Bible, the Torah and the Koran
The Sanskrit ignored or thrown on the heap
The band of sanctimonious castes are replete
With man-made saints and devotees

Hawking salvation on gilded pulpits or shrines
Faking miracles in confounding gibberish and rhymes
Pundits line their pockets by passing trays
Convert tithes to imposing mansions

Adorning themselves in the latest fashions
Spreading their wings and flying in private jets
Procured and maintained by the duped sects
Totally abandoning the virtue of humility
Turning their backs to that of honesty
Against the likenesses of the Image of God
They file for tax exemptions
But without shame tax their congregations

Claiming it all converts to spiritual redemption
Invalidating the purpose of being made
In the likeness of the "Image of God
Dragging The Holy name in the mud
But God cannot be mocked!—
Religious corruption creates the air of sanctity
Which belies its true identity
Conferring holiness to one of its clones

But Holiness is due to God alone!
Each preacher, sect and branch
Puts its captives in a trance
Each brand of faith or religion
Prophesying spiritual concessions
Blackmailing their adherents with doctored scoops
Of differing versions of the Divine Truth
Resorting to murders, incarcerations or conquests

Like the Crusade, the jihad, the inquisition and the rest
Birthing and mid-wifing terrorism round the world
Orchestrated by egotistic manmade accords
In opposition to the natural nurturing Love
Of those made in the likeness of the Image of God
The gullible adherents are corrupted
With bribes of assurances of salvation
From all their transgressions

Unconditionally saved from eternal damnation
By the blood of Jesus as from calf or the fowl
Making God a raving vampire
In the vein of the gods of old empires
With medicine men as the umpires
Believers are turned into apes
Drinking from the stupefying rays
Of the jaunty drag queens in robes or paints

Who say one thing on the pulpit and shrines
And another behind the blinds
The calls for life long celibacy
A downright blasphemy
That adulterates the doting clients
The ornate cathedrals or shrines
Morphed into flirting grounds and tourist attractions
The confessions and canonisations

Hubristic assaults on the supremacy of God
Highjacking Divine prerogatives
Claiming equality of man and his Creator

Arrogating to man a status outside his bounds
Conferring Divinity to man
And yet not Omniscient, Omnipotent and Omnipresent!

B. MATRIMONIAL CORRUPTION

Matrimonial corruption drives the nail deep
Its victims have nightmares in their sleep
It makes its preys junkies in the trade of the flesh
With pretentious airs more or less
Converts its candidates to perpetual gamblers
In the slippery court of drifters
Battling with inescapable escapades
Of emotional piracies and rapes

Delusions and deceptions
Harassments and seductions
Perverting sincerity
Depreciating morality
It drags lives through labyrinths of intrigues
That turn marriages into contracts of greed
Breaking the laws of give and take
Creating a world of break and take

Refuting the oath of a man to a woman
And that of the woman to her dear man
To love and to hold till death do us part...
Couples are broken apart
Destroying the family pact
The union bound by God
Becomes one not bound by love
But clings on financial bonds

That hawk moral frauds
With arms and legs as divorce costs
Infidelity lurks in every closet
Breaking down the matrimonial concept
The man playing the masculine card with a rod
Sucking up the union's free fresh blood
Triggering off matrimonial blood clots
Clogging up the woman's sacred call

For her's is not a bed-mate role
Her's is not a door-mat role
Her's is not a chattel role
Neither is it a dominating role
Nor is it a submissive role
Her delicate frame defines her path
Her sensitivity gives strength to her homely tasks
Her heightened intuition backs her stance

Her's is not to compete with her man
Her's it is to lead his band
To inspire the dreams he tills in the fields
Her's is not to provide for their breeds
But her's it is to ennoble the yields
Of all their matrimonial seeds
Her humble disposition sets her tone
As the guardian priestess of the home

The male figure is an open book
And cannot be mistaken for a snook
The broad top and narrow bottom
Were not made for picking cotton

His it is to wrestle with the winds
His it is to tame the fields
His it is to milk nature's gifts
His it is to be the head on the wife's neck

But single parenthood has changed the rules
Breeding delinquent Robin Hoods
The natural balance lost in the broods
Suicides and addictions haunt the grounds
Where insecurity breeds gangsters hounds
Immorality in all guises
Seep through the rank and file
Of the victims in their daily lives

Child molestation, incest and rape
Human trafficking and kidnapping in the chase
Harlotry and pimping also in trail
The child in this haunted isle
Armed with one wing cannot really fly
High enough to hide
From the persistent ringing of bells
Coming from the nearby juvenile jails

C. POLITICAL CORRUPTION

Political corruption thrives on incentives
It wears the guise of sham objectives
Drowning the conscience, selling poise
Obliterating fairness, bagging the spoils

Elections manipulated, often times rigged!
Ballots are doctored to favour the rich
Voters are suppressed and their rights ditched
All subverting Nature's Bills of Rights

Precincts are changed to swell some polls
Money speaking much louder than the folks
Dirty hands washing much dirtier hands
All in the collective amnesia
Of the virtues of transparency and honesty
As the likenesses of the Image of God
Candidates characters shammed
Parties undermining other parties with their fans

Parties going to bed with the system
Not with the people who voted for the system
All subverting Nature's Bills of Rights
Mandatory to all who live their lives
As likenesses of the Image of God
Without which the affairs of our world
Will increasingly go from bad to worse
Until we reverse our loveless course

To collude and confuse has become the motto
To divide and rule the winning mojo
Promises made are not delivered
Demagogues feathering their bulging nests
And the people beat their heavy chests
Seeming unable to change their fates
In the face of blatant civil rights rapes
All subverting Nature's Bills ofRight

D. GENDER CORRUPTION

Comes gender corruption
This has bred much confusion
Homosexuals and lesbians make confessions
Claiming their rights and demanding concessions
Prudence and shame are thrown to the dust
The sense of right wrestling with wrong
Mandatory to all who live their lives
As true likenesses of the Image of God

Men claim to have been women wronged
Cutting and planting body parts where they don't belong
Confusing facts with fantasy
Putting their lives in jeopardy
Questioning the reason why it is vouched
That homo-sapiens eat food with their mouths
And void body wastes through the lower gates
No matter if the gender is male or female

Women claim to be men
Men doing the same
Men dress like women in the same vein
Women dress like men doing their jobs
Losing their abilities to light the spiritual torch
Men act like women and speak like them
Emasculating manhood, damning their sperms
Women tattoo just like men

Turning both into an artist's pallet
Men build bodies and form hard blades
Of pumped muscles they later hate
Harming their bodies for self-consuming fame

Women body build just like men
Clamping womanhood into an iron cage
Women kick-box with flying braids
Punching womanhood in the proverbial face

Hanging noble womanhood on iron rails
Locking her priestess-hood in security jails
Clogging mankind's spiritual life-support
Other corruptions abound
Which are equally profound
All of which have laid the ground
For the overall degeneration
Of humanity's moral obligations

E. AGRICULTURAL CORRUPTION

The misappropriation of God's creation
Executed with the ill-conceived intension
Of controlling God's instituted operations
Is precipitating fearful repercussions
In all the field of our daily activities
Agricultural corruption has known repercussions
On the perpetration of the human population
Seeding all forms of genetic incursions

Into culinary recipes of dangerous concoctions
With ingredients sautéed in false genetic emulsions
Hormones fed to the fauna and flora
Creating food toxic situations in the world arena

Cloning animals for meat and fashion
Clothes, shoes, boots for collection
Brings to the climax the aberration
Of the uncontrolled adventurer

The temptress and goddess of no restraint
On the freedom of all expressions
For the sky is said to be the limit
So in misplaced philanthropy
Misguided pity and generosity
Charitable organisations pump virgin lands
With genetically altered seeds and feeds
For bumper yields with double edged blades

Cause speedy returns artificially induced
Have meantime bred gluttonous guts
Whose greedy intents birthed abhorrent results
Distorting the natural balance in gestation and yield
Hormone inflated products now swarm the fields
Contaminating everything we eat
From eggs in their shells
And chicken in their nests

To goats and cows and all the meat
Fish and chips and mutton from sheep
Fruits and drinks in bottles or cans
With the misleading names of their brands
Legumes and roots fresh or frozen
Vegetables of all descriptions glistening
Locally grown or imported
Most are now genetically corrupted

Leaving humanity swimming blind
In the deep ocean of uncertainty
With undetectable viral infirmity
Lurking behind all the popular innovations
In the growth of food productions
Greatly enhanced with GMOs
Claiming unqualified advancement
In humanity's investment in itself

F. MEDICAL CORRUPTION

Medical malpractices numb the heart
Pharmaceutical giant constellations
Drive their satellites into black holes of desolation
Their tantalising glows create antidotes for ransoms
Blackmailing the desperate sick
With insensitive conceit
Hiking prices, making claims
For solutions not sustained

Sending many to their early graves
Cause costs don't convert to cures
Nor brand names permit censors
Specialists fake fees for fake oracles
Hospitals exaggerate bills
Ignoring the truly sick
Driving the poor to die in desolate pits
Dangerous drugs hawked on the streets

Turning junkies into human freaks
In the financial nuptial romance
Between life insurance and health insurance

Masquerading as social benefits bedmates
Their tentacles feeding on the disparate dying
Auctioning drugs that cause addiction
The pharmacies jumping for the scoop
Lobbying the leaders who lobby the brood

G. FINANCIAL CORRUPTION

Financial corruption crowns them all
With banks and treasuries coining the fraud
And money as the root of all ills
Is choking mankind with an iron grip
Turning nations against nations
Factions against factions
Village against another
Even one gang against another

Brothers against brothers
Sisters against sisters
Neighbours against neighbours
Children against parents
Business against business
Governments against the people
The world against itself
With one aim alone—making more more money

Money has become our God!
Making us do only what it wants
Destroying our will to conform
To the Will of He who made us all

We work for money from night till dawn
Groping in the dark sick and worn
Labouring with cracking bones and joint
Pursuing money till the day we die

With all our wit and all our might
We dance for money
We kill for money
We lie for money every hour everyday
No matter what may be at stake
We sell our lives for the indispensable fluke
Waking each day striving for the ruse
We make right wrong and wrong right

And get away with it, with it on our side
Cause it rules the world in any name
With all the accompanying grace and fame
The popularity and accolades and grace
The pomp and power and fanfares
That come with its entourage
With money we can do anything
With money we can go anywhere

With money we can say anything
Cause money has bought everything
Casting all in its own image
Of materiality, insensitivity and decay
Depositing all in the investment banks
That hoard the fruit we die to sow
Swelling the bankers' portfolios
Laundering monies, counterfeiting currencies

Driving borrowers into bankruptcies
Manipulating and hiking rates
Speculating and gambling with tainted chips
Touting gains in statement slips
The treasury their national counterpart
With the powerful whips of the land
Levying taxes for spurious ends
Pouring revenues down their own drains

All against the rule of Love
For all mankind made in the Likeness
Of the Image of God
Whose actions should be pure
Yet tax returners make false claims
Businesses and institutions dodging audits
Aided and abetted by a network of bandits
Bribing clients with some periodic treats

Insurance companies their wedded grooms
Capitalise on our fears of doom
Life insurance become debt incurrence
The companies refuting their bound assurance
Turning deaf ears to clients in their need
Denying them timely helps when they plead
Litigating them with fraudulent counter pleads
Adding insults to injuries

Mesmerised by the lure of money
Burying our consciences in the coffins
Of deluding material well being
Clouding our minds to what tomorrow may bring

To all of us on earth still living
Created by God with His Pure Love
In the likeness of His own Image of Love
Not in the likeness of the image of gold

H. CORPORATE CORRUPTION

Corruption nests in corporations like a snake
Slithering through the corporate ladder and base
With foaming venom in its long tongue
it's serpentine mind firmly set
On swelling it's guts by swallowing all it tastes
Consumers and competitors are its baits
Expansion and profit being the stake
In the rat race that consumes its days

CEOs do all it takes
To grow their stakes and make them great
It does not matter what is at stake
They bribe politicians with financial cakes
Go any length to secure their base
Lobby legislators for personal gains
Letting money not Love take the reins
All taking place at the consumers expense

Who they should love as they love themselves
Mindful of the law of what you sow you reap
For all made in the Likeness of the Image of God
But in the delusion of all that is material

They intimidate competitors
And make nefarious deals
That satisfy their greed
Falsify their earnings, cooking their books

To pay less taxes than their cooks
They claim exempts and privileges
For philanthropic companies
That do not exist
All against the nature of those
Made in the likeness of the Image of God
Consumers ride on financial rollercoasters
With chattering teeth from their high velocity greed

Hoarding goods they hardly need
With costs escalating and commodities faked
And consumers financially raped
Goods sold with glamorous commercial scoops
With women as baits on their fishing hooks
Serving as nothing but commercial tools
Casting women in falsified moulds
Of mere properties in commercial holds

I. PARENTAL CORRUPTION

Paediatric corruption strikes the earliest blow
Parents forcing children their love to show
With unsolicited fondling they much resist
The roused emotions of the physical kiss

Undermine their embryonic free wills
Corrupting their pallets with the conventional drill
Which at first they vehemently oppose
But finally helplessly condone

Because the parents insist
Assaulting their young libidinous instincts
Which later impairs their sexual habits
Piggybacked by the corporate bourgeoisie
Whose pockets burst on every Fair or Halloween
While the fate of children's masticating tools
Are lost in candies vending booths
Piñata bursts and other fiestas

The sugar hyped confectionary drills
Make them financial guinea pigs
The dentists claim their shares in the feast
As the sweetened palates crave for more
The corporate gluttons glamorise their whore
And the hooked connoisseurs fall victims to the ruse
Spending life times battling the attendant bruises
At the dentists' fancy booths or clinics

Equipped with the doctors's spells and gimmicks
With big holes in their leaking pockets
Parents imposing their wishes on their children
Assault their natural self esteem
Delaying their timely engagements
In the drive for self-development
Triggering rebellions and manic depressions
Leading to heightened frustrations

To fears of failures and loss of steam
In their developmental skills and dreams
Losing the power to make life's decisions
In the face of challenging oppositions
The male having hen-pecked inclinations
With crippling psychic implications
The females additionally suffer abuses
Spousal or social some simply confused

Gender related or work related
Unable to stand on their own feet
All dependent and insecure
Leaning on others for support
Parents or states become ports of call
When life's drizzles turn to storms
Fear gains advantage at any challenge
Obstructing the progression of progress

Planting failure in all so distressed
Brought about by parental power abuse
Where there should have been mutual respect
Between offsprings and parents
Based on the loving expression
Of nature's demands in the exercise
Of free wills as the decisive tool
For all made in God's Loving Image

J. ENTERTAINMENT CORRUPTION

Our entertainment industries
Run the most glamorous tapestries
Of life corrupting pageantries

Boasting of pockets bursting with shows
On screens, theatres and community groves
Sentencing consciences to the death role
Creating a viral virtual world of impostors
On stilts for shoes and bogus sun-shades

The industries sensational simulations
Of facts and fictions in wild confusion
Dreams and soul-searching fantasies
Have inadvertently hyped our grievances
Inspiring and buttressing the negative nuances of life
Their glamour lure all to pompous drills
That hold us spellbound with reverting thrills
That desensitise with styles and skills the industries instil

These genres of entertainments
Open wide doors to the dark aisles of merriment
They breed self-glory and pride bred predicaments
Creating demigods and goddesses
Glamourising all forms of indecencies
Glorifying vanity and villainy
Sending the world round the bend
Stripping the world of all sense of shame

Star aspirants relinquish their values
Even their bodies to make the news
Some change their looks
To remain in the books
Some abandon home to look for fake thrones
Some their moral integrity vying for roles
Just to make names
In the world's halls of fame

There is no policing
In the tension stoked industry
To prevent abuses sexual or social
Nor power abuses emotional or verbal
Political, religious or otherwise
Glamorised or criticised in their virtual world
Inadvertently escalating deviant clienteles
With malicious eyes all round the globe

The entire globe is a gorge on the whole
With the glamor of the silver screens in control
Round the globe actors preen themselves
Like peacocks with airs and means
Technology exceeding itself in the captivating scenes
With the effects that affect human races to the extreme
And make-beliefs that indoctrinate
Corrupting more than it inspires all the mates

The trends of violent actions on screens
The trends of sensual actions on screens
The trends of wicked actions on screens
The trends of oppressive actions on screens
Of suppressive actions on screens
Of dictatorial actions on screens
Of immoral actions on screens
Have globalised the industry's indoctrinating machines

Wreaking havoc on humanity's genes
The glamorised portrayal of drug addiction
Has raised the toll of the affliction
Among the dis-enfranchised population

Of the have nots in all nations
Who have lost the hope of rising
Beyond their restricted settings
Yet wishing that things were a lot different

Like Father Like Son

Nothing happens without a rap
On the cosmic map of infinite Love
For its energy composes and governs all
Linking one creature with the other
To forge an unbroken eternal chain
Of pure life-giving vibrations
Of the upbuilding sparks of God's Love
In all the creatures of the world

Though the chain has been broken a million times
With mankind wallowing in muddy side tracks
The subliminal links of all humanity
Makes all accountable for our infirmity
Shareholders in the endemic infections
Of the epidemics of perversions
In our shared daily experiences
With the bonding forces of Love

Making imitation natural to all living things
As we affect and reflect each other
In all fields of human endeavour
From infancy to puberty
From puberty to maturity
Imitation is our silent teacher
So when we choose our different leaders
We do so in that natural law

Let us then see the parts we played
In making walking epitomes
Of our haunting woes
For the saga of the time
Prints the nature of our crimes
On the front pages of the cosmic 'Times'
Tolling the sum of our contributions
To the confronting repercussions

For there is no rain without a cloud
No smoke without a fire!...
The smokes from our leaders
Signal the fires in our camps
For they demonstrate the ills we have
They amplify the hates we have
They exemplify the bigotry we have
Because we are both instinctive copycats

So we both share the guilt
They postulate the indignity we have
Promulgate the hypocrisy we have
Extrapolate on the biases we have
Exaggerate the phobias we have
Intensify the prejudices we have
Justify the greed we have
Dramatise the felonies we commit

Because we are both instinctive copycats
We both share the guilt
The school teacher who bullies
Does so because others do so

The farmer who adulterates his produce
Does so because others do so
The manufacturer who does the same
Does so because others do so
They all share the guilt

The law enforcement officer who bre
The writer who plagiarises
The athlete who takes performance d
The fighter who fakes his punches
The student who cheats in exams
All do so because they are all instinc
They all share the guilt

The child molester does so
Because many others do so
The rapist does so
Because many others do so
The murderer does so
Because others do so
The parent who neglects his or her child
All do so because they are instinctive copycats

They all share the guilt
The attorney who falsifies to win a case
Does so because other lawyers do so
The man who scams does so
Because many others do so
Those who rob or defraud do so
Because many others do so
People who fake their identities do so

Because others do so and share the guilt
People who conspire against others do so
Because others do so
People who retaliate do so
Because others do so
People who wear designers clothes do so
People who become gang members do so
Because their peers or friends do so and share the guilt

People who gossip do so
Because others do so so
Men who talk lewd locker-room talks do so
Because others do so
People who womanise do so
Because many other men do so
People who prostitute do so
Because others do so and all share the guilt

People who steal and shop-lift do so
Because they see others do so
The youths become insubordinate
Because they copy their spicy mates
People become drug addicts
Because their friends float in the mist
People become virtually evil
In this perverted rather than inspiring mimicry

Igniting infernos of chaos internally and globally
Diplomatic equity hang on thin accords
Climate change policies fanning more discords
Because lawmakers are at loggerheads

Protecting their vested interests
Economic climates round the world
Sway on cyclonic concords
Because of selfish patriotism

That cares little for the underdogs of globalism
Fanning more chaos and rebellions
Destroying human relations
Short circuiting true progress
Disparity in wealth breeding civil unrest
Uncontrollable high cost of living
Breeding banditry and joblessness
Escalating crimes and homelessness

The flaring up of insurgencies
Of rebellions, coup d'état and protests
The ballooning of crimes and neglect
Of refugees fleeing from raging wars
One thing leading to other political and moral flaws
Because we live in a world of cause and effects...
There is a Donald Trump who won some votes
There is a Hillary who missed the boat

Nature herself set the rules
Night gives birth to day
We sleep, we wake
Unless we sleep in death
There is warmth because there is heat
There is snow because of freezing air or winter
There are floods because of excess water
There are droughts for lack of water

We are alive to strive for spiritual maturity
Propagate God's Love and take good care
Of what He has placed in our care
We came into this realm as He planned
And His guiding laws for ever stand
Resisting alterations of His modus-operandi
For joyful achievements of lasting peace and prosperity
For all the races of humanity

But we have never walked the walk
And the fruits of our monumental flaws
Have not been to our advantage
But with false indignation we vociferate
Blaming our neighbours or God for our fates
Rather than accepting the tale-tell fact
That we have been caught in the rebellious act
Of stepping out of God's laws of Living with Love

Out of tune with the original song
Out of sync with the vibrations of the planet of Love
Which then responds with cleansing forces
We put it down to our inquisitive selves
Our tastes for the exotic and the strange
Our hunger for innovation and change
Or simply to boldly challenge
God's tough-Love in every way

We brew ideas with our imaginative skills
Creating artificial realities and still
Right now we have ended up cold
Running around with hearts of stone

Refuting all the glaring signs that show
That nature's loom is froth with doom
Cause its systems firmly refuse
All the corruptive elements we have devised

In place of the original proven joyride
Of the invincible Power of Love

*P*art *Two*

Damage Control

A. The Phoenix Arising

The defying smoke of smothered hopes
Stretch out into the horizon in all zones
Reaching for a spark of the quickening flame
That flickers and hums and never ever wanes
The ambers of embodied Ulysses
Still glimmer in the human species
Cause that which induced our lethargy
Dramatising our myopic apathy

Making us so self-serving
Is under a revolutionary siege
By the incorruptible power of unconditional Love
Urging all humanity to change their hearts
So they can change their identity caps
To bear the shining logos of universal love
As they sing the Life-Giving Love songs
With the words that say:

Share rather than hoard
Give rather than take
Forgive rather than revenge
Support rather than suppress
Encourage rather than discourage
Cooperate rather than terrorise
Inspire rather than deride
Praise rather than disgrace

Contribute rather than disparage
Trust rather than distrust
Respect rather than suspect
Integrate rather than segregate
Restrain rather than instigate
Liberate rather than enslave
Admire rather than detest
Include rather than exclude

Placate rather than incense
Share rather than monopolise
Befriend rather than antagonise
Dance rather than fight
Bring laughter rather than tears
In the eyes of all of the human races
And make God's kingdom come on earth
As the likenesses of the Image of God

Not put our future at stake
In the scheme that God has put in place
Which does not buckle with human mistakes
In all our efforts to take all and dominate
Rather than giving that we may receive
And always dividing to rule
That causes mankind to repeatedly flounder
Rather than uniting in order to conquer

B. *Applying The Power Of Love*

As we are made the human copies
Of God's Holy Image of Love
And as likes attract their own kind
Love will play its natural role
Of letting Love attract Love once more
In the hearts of rulers, masters and servants
The hearts of the woman and the man
The hearts of all humankind

As we are made in the human likeness
Of the Image of God in His eternal Love
Whose whole energy is of Living Love
Anything out of this ocean of Love
Is doused in the essence of that love
Nothing else but that Living Love
That Life Giving and sustaining Love
Is the restoration joyride for all the world

Nothing else but that Living Love
Can successfully direct all operations
When we do anything in God's Creation
Without Love as the motive power
We therefore put our lives in danger
We therefore play with burning fire
We therefore deny ourselves the only power
That conducts life's wire and fibre

When we do anything in God's Creation
Without Love as the motive power
Things and nations fall apart
Cause we fail to play our given parts
In the nature of all true archetypes
Of the likeness of the image of the Living God
But have turned around and bitten the finger
Of He Whose Love is our Life-Giving Power

Have counterfeited that power in us
Have ignored that power in us
Have misused that power in us
Have substituted that power of Love
With powers that destroy our Lives
Like hate and greed and lust
Like prejudice spiced with villainy and force
Like all the things we do without Love

Compromising the Love in us
Contorting the Love in us
Debasing the Love in us
Demeaning the Love in us
Disfiguring the Love in us
Degrading the Love in us
Disabling the Love in us
All to pay the impending costs

But Loving Others As We Love Ourselves
Will drive away all our inhibitions
Will surely banish all our hesitations
In doing what is good in any situation

Giving us the vicarious satisfaction
Of being good to our own very essence
Helping us make all the difference
Cause Love alone has all the means

To meet all humanity's needs
In the cities or the hamlets
In the villages or the mighty palaces
In any human habitat around the globe....
There is a new Love story to be told
A new battle story that is very old
The new fierce battle that the magnetic role
Of Living Love can play with pragmatism

As permissiveness jeers at conformism
And indignation battles with confusion
In the minds of the old and the young
In the fight for right and wrong
Now raging in the heart of the sane
With blinding migraine on fatigued brains
Seeking to change the current trends
Of dangerous epidemics of unrests

We rouse the muses to join us
In singing the liberating song of Love
In every note and every phrase
With every breath it may take
To say the word -LOVE
Love, Love, Living Love
Is the only answer for it all
The only answer to forestall

The acceleration of our pending collapse
The love that hears all
In the likeness of the Image of God
Not just some people
The love that listens to all
Not only to some people
The love that gives to all
Not just to some people

The love that stands by all
Not just by some people
The love that speaks good of all
Not only of some people
The love that cares for all
Not just for some people
The love that protects all
In the likeness of the Image of God

The Love that defends all
Not any special ones
The Love that provides for all
Not any special ones
The Love that helps all
Not just some ones
The Love that believes in all
In the likeness of the Image of God

The Love that cooperates with all
Not any preferred ones
The Love that values all
Not just the special ones

That does what is good for all
Not just for the special ones
That empathises with all
In the likeness of the Image of God

Love that is kind to everyone
Not just the chosen ones
Love that thinks well of everyone
Not just the chosen ones
Love that sees only what is good in everyone
Not just in the chosen ones
Love that provides for everyone
In the likeness of the Image of God

Love that empowers everyone
Not just the chosen ones
Love that respects everyone
Not just the chosen ones
Love that makes all happy
Not just some chosen ones
Love that rewards everyone
In the likeness of the Image of God

The Love that loves all without exception
In the likeness of the Image of God
Anything outside that denies Love
Anything outside that denies God
Anything outside that falsifies our true identity
Which falsifies our natural abilities
Denying us the true activities
Of the creative attributes of the Love in us

Anything outside that defines man
As a mythical troll
Trapped in his own mortal hole
For God is Love who gave life to everyone
Not to chosen ones
His Love gave life to all the beasts
Not just to some chosen beasts
His Love gave life to all fishes

Not just to some fishes
His Love gave life to all the trees
Not to some chosen trees....
All denials of God is futile
All scientific refutations sterile
His energy sparks that we can never contrive
Form Love's building energy particles
Which science can never replicate

C. Commitment To Living Love

God's Love is all embracing
Controlling all in the universe
Mankind by now should come to know
Who is truly in control
Of our destiny and our roles
In making the world a happy home
With all the benevolent gifts bestowed
On all the inhabitants of the globe

The birds, the fishes and all the trees
The animals in the forests, in holes and hills
The demeanour of the weather, from day to day
From month to month and year to year
From seasons to season without ceasing
Century to century, never changing
Epoch to epoch and age to age
All playing their roles in humanity's fate

All tallying humanity's scores
In the cosmic chart of universal Love
To maintain equilibrium in the vibration
Of all the components of the mechanism of Creation
The lack of the maintenance and flow
Of the energy of Love in our world
Has frequently caused a breach in the Love circulation
Leading to disasters of cataclysmic proportions

The chaos from lovelessness in our world today
Compels the need for a necessary change
For rebuilding our lives with the missing Love
In all its universal ramifications
To restore the vanishing shadows
Of all that makes us human beings
And reignite the paramount commitment
Of serving God with all our Loving endowments

Using love as the universal currency
For all made in the likeness of God
Restoring peace among all men
In all communities of the earth
So let's recommit ourselves to Love
In every way, every time and everywhere
The human races live and operate
So was it meant to be in the first place

Let's recommit to Love in Equality
To restore racial and social Harmony
Let's recommit to Love in Honesty
To restore unwavering dependability
Let's recommit to Love in Equity
To restore unbiased Justice
Let's recommit to Love in Sincerity
To restore enduring Integrity

Let's recommit to Love in Humility
To restore deserving Honour
Let's recommit to Love in Truth
To restore unshakable Trust
Let's recommit to Love in Compassion
To restore subliminal Empathy
Let's recommit to Love in Giving
To restore Kindness and Love for all

D. Acting With Love

Let's refuse to scam
To stamp out deceit
Let's not con
To reinstate human dignity
Let's not defraud
To build a strong economy
Let's not cheat
To reestablish honesty

Let's not steal
To put our natural gifts to good use
Let's not undermine others
To reestablish unity
Let's not vilify
To spread heart felt happiness
Let's not accuse
To grace our world with lasting peace

Let's not abuse anyone
To entrench tolerance and respect
Let's not mentally abuse anyone
To eliminate inferiority complexes
Let's not physically abuse anyone
To eliminate violence
Let's not verbally abuse anyone
To prevent fights

Let's not racially or sexually abuse anyone
To eliminate phobias
Let's not abuse politically
To avoid oppression or suppression
Let's not abuse ethically
To eliminate immorality of any kind
Let's not abuse spiritually
To prevent extremism and fanaticism

Nor condemn but encourage
To promote all progress with Love
At work or play
At home or away
In the office or the traffic
In the store or the clinic
At the pool or school
In the city or the village

In our deeds our thoughts and our words
For the good of everyone
At the club or the pub
The gym or the stadium
The hotel or the motel
At the hair dresser or the dressmaker
At the court-room or ball-room
In the bedroom or living room

In the lobby or classroom
In stores or factories
On the road or the streets
In the high rise or basement

In the mansion or the hut
In jail or on bail
Oppressed or liberated
At the games or in bed

On the bus or the train
At the show or the fair
Letting Love manifest in all we do
In making the car or the boat
In navigating on land or sea
In the kitchen or the field
In the city or the village
In the night or in the day

In High or low spirit
Drowning or floating
Holding on to Love losing or winning
For Love will always win
Failing or succeeding
For Love never fails
Accepted or rejected
For Love loves all

Betrayed or rebuked
For Love sees only what is good
Let us make the changes we need
By planting well-meant seeds
In words, thoughts and deeds
To forge more benevolent boomerangs
Returning to free our world
From the forebodings of recriminations

E. Turning The New Leaf

Corruption carved what's on our boomerangs
To stand for the emblems of our time
We are reaping our fruits duly ripe
The emblems on the boomerangs
Break down all what is now at stake
To help us not repeat the good old mistakes
For our own good let us let go
The loveless things our leaders have done

From now on and never go back
Let go those things our leaders have done
To make us cover our eyes in shame
Let them go ourselves and never go back
Let go those things our leaders have said
To make us shut our ears in disbelief
Let them go ourselves and never go back
Let go those things our leaders have said

To make us hold our breaths in shock
Let them go ourselves and never go back
Let go all things our leaders do
To make us grind our teeth with disgust
Let them go ourselves and never go back
Those things our leaders do
To make us stamp our feet in condemnation
Let them go ourselves and never go back

Those things our leaders do
To make us beat our chests in pain
Let them go ourselves from now on
And never go back
Those things our leaders have done
To make us bite our tongues in horror
Let them go ourselves from now on
And never go back

Let them go from now on
And never go back
Let go those things our leaders do
To make us shake our heads in disbelief
Let them go ourselves from now on
And never go back
Those things our leaders do
To make us gnash our teeth in despair

Let them go ourselves from now on
And never go back
Those things our leaders do
To make us roll our eyes in disgust
Let them go ourselves from now on
And never go back
Let go those things our leaders do
To make us drop our jaws in disbelief

Those things our leaders do
To make us bow our heads in sorrow
Those things they do that we do
Let them go ourselves from now on

And never go back
Those loveless things they have said
That we still say
Let them go ourselves from now on

Let them go from now on
Let them go from now on
And never go back
All loveless causes they have supported
That we still support
Let them go from now on
Let them go from now on
And never go back

Those things at which they have connived
At which we still connive
Let them all go from now on
And never go back
Never go back
Never try to go back
From now on
Those nefarious acts they have covered up

That we still cover up
Let them go
And never go back
The crimes that they have committed
That we still commit
Day and night undercover and out of sight
Let them go
Let them go

Let them go

And never, ever go back
All the things we know we should never have done
That we still do now
Let them all go from now on
And never, ever go back
If we want real unity and progress
For a people "under God!"

A people made in the likeness
Of the loving Image of God
Bearing all the attributes of Love in us
For our successful experiences
With all the other creatures
That share the earth's treasures
Leaving nothing out of the Love exchange
That keeps everything sane

For nature's cuisine inspires good chefs
And its pantry is fully stocked with the best
For nourishing its precious guests
All we need to do
Is make authentic stews
Chosen from its nurturing culinary books
Only then can we be poison proof
Only then can damages be controlled

Making our beings glow
And our talents unfold
Common sense dictating common grace
Common grace infecting all the human race

The primordial laws being quite fair
Having trees grow on land not in mid air
The sun to shine in the day not in the night
And man to live by Love alone in all his plights

Deviations from these norms
Distort and deform all that had been formed
And the smooth mechanisms of Creation
Convulse against all the corruptions
In relentless emissions and eruptions
To cleanse creation of our negative effusions
And restore cosmic harmony
In the orchestra of our Loving universe

It responds to synchronised melodies
Of Loving anthems in perfect harmony
But alas we have not synchronised nor harmonised
But brutally scrambled and jarred all the notes
Now there is cacophony from all around the globe!
The music we now play perjures our souls
The music we now play weakens our hearts
The music we now play distorts our lives

Brothers and sisters let us open our eyes
Brothers and sisters let us open our ears
Brothers and sisters let us open our hearts
To harken to the sublime call of Love
From the gentle voices of our grieving souls
As the true Children of God
Longing to share the love of which we are made
The love so perversive and restorative

What we now need is the change of hearts
Not a change of governments anywhere
What we now need is a change of hearts
Not a change of political parties anywhere
What we now need is a change of hearts
Not a change of the economy anywhere
What we now need is a change of hearts
To change our looming, gloomy self-destructive fate

F. Why Love?

God is Love, that is why
His Love is Life, that is why
Living is loving, that is why
Loving is living, that is why
God made everything out of Himself
That is why
Giving His Love to everything in Creation
That is why

He Willed everything by His Love
Our words are charged with His Love
Our thoughts are charged with His Love
Our deeds are charged with His Love
His Love maintains everything
His Love controls everything
His Love sustains everything
His Love is in everything

His Love presides over everything
His Love dictates and supports all
His Love governs and nurtures all
His Love guides and protects all
It is indestructible
It is inexhaustible
It encapsulates all that there is
That is why

The air we breathe is made of That Love
The water we drink is made of that Love
The land, the ocean and the seas
The flora, the fauna, the seen and unseen
All took form when He gave the fiat
"Let there be Light!" and there was Light!
Out of His Life-Giving Love
The atoms, neutrons, protons and all energy spores

Shot out from His Love radiating core
To be the building blocks of all the worlds
All things react to That Energy
All things thrive in that Energy
All things cannot be without that Energy
Trees and grasses die without that Energy
Animals and all die
Without That Holy Energy of Love

Humans malfunction and die
By misusing That Energy
Humans kill each other
By damning That Energy
Humans commit all the crimes
By corrupting That Energy
Humans oppress their fellow men
By stamping down That Energy

Humans become dictators
By restricting That Energy
Leaders deceive their people
By distorting That Energy

We misrule our people
By suppressing That Energy
Plunging us headlong into endless wars
Never having peace in our world

Peace is an attribute of that Energy
Compassion is an attribute of that Energy
Forgiveness is an attribute of that Energy
Helping is an attribute of that Energy
Without that Energy nothing can survive
That Energy is the elixir of Life!
A child grows in that Energy
Insects respond to that Energy

A dog wags his tail with That Energy
All animals respond to That Energy
And humans yearn for That Energy
Write 99% of songs about Love lost,
Hidden or found or given away
While That Energy they so much crave
Awaits their call in their DNA
Awaits their call every split second of the day

Responds to their call at work or play
Responds to their call in life's every phase
From night till dawn, every step of the way
Every circumstance no matter the case
Awaits to be summoned first
Least in the carnal only way
Every minute of the day
Every second we are awake

Cause it is in our every vein
Our every artery and every cell
And it is eager to serve in every way
Cause It is made to behave that way
Every man and every woman
Every child, boy or girl
Is under compulsion to express that Holy Love
It is at the beck and call of of us all

Every fish in the waters of the earth
Every beast on land on our earth
It is in the sand, the rock, the stars above
In everything under the sun
It is in the water we drink and the food we eat
The flora and fauna and the air we breath
Fulfilling the Will of their Giver to us all
For living our lives with the power of Love

The Love supply is in-exhaustible
It's persuasive ploys irresistible
Like a river it's water must flow
No matter the path it takes to do so
To hoard the Love for the sake of one
Is like wearing a straight jacket and trying to run
But blocked brooks find new routes
To make their ways to the end they must pursue

So when we fail to love as we should
We are compelled to love as we must
Love then turns to addiction and lust
Obsession and elation with aggression, the lot

Transposed to negative expressions
Contradicting Love's good intentions
But the pressure of Love from its source
Never abates but urges all that lie in its course

To express the Love poured into us
Every split second without a fuss
With no discrimination nor hesitation
Setting everything in constant motion
Its radiation spans the universe
Creating forms in different spheres
Never deviating from its benevolent cause
To ensure successes in all its course

The power of Love activates all that is good
And shuns all not in its book
So we must play it by its rule
If we truly want our own good
For all exist for nothing but Love
All expects nothing else but Love
All contains nothing else but Love
And to live is therefore to love

Cause it encapsulates all life
And manifests all virtues
Love is in Justice
Love is in Purity
It is in kindness
It is in generosity
It is in compassion
It is in tolerance

It is in faithfulness
Love is in forgiveness
Love is in mercy
Love is in chastity
Love is in diligence
Love is in perseverance
Love is in patience
In all that enhances righteous living

In the environment of harmony
The environment of security
The environment of peace
In all that nurtures man spiritually and materially
Feeding him with sublime happiness
But, Love, the mother of all that lives
The indispensable attributes of all that exists
Now stands abused by callous humanity

Traded as a carnal commodity
Utterly misunderstood and bastardised
Degraded to the level of a trading tool
To offer whomsoever we may choose
Restraining its captive powers
Curtailing its universal grandeur
Pampering it in carnal boudoirs
Leaving it to languish in privacy alone

Dispensing it to our bedmates with hopes
Of satisfying our lusts
Not for dispensing pure Love to all
In giving with love to all

In working with love for all
In ruling with love for all
In thinking of love for all
In doing everything with love for all

Our corruption of the expression of Love
Has left us bereft of the benevolent effects
Of its generative rays of upbuilding energy
Originating from God's core of Love
We are bereft of the nurturing power of Love
We are bereft of the uplifting power of Love
We are bereft of the healing power of Love
We are bereft of the unifying power of Love

We are bereft of peace
We are bereft of happiness
At home and workplaces
In the fields and offices
In entertainment and government
In all areas of daily living
Prompting serious soul searching
If we truly care for all that is still living

G. The Arms Of Love

Because "Everything is Love"
And "Love governs all existence"
As confirmed in "In The light of Truth-
The Grail Message" by Abd Ru Shin!
Without the constant interchange
Of this energy from one entity to another
In whatever the position or location
Whatever the time or condition

Whatever the problem or circumstance
Whatever the relationship or the distance
The organisation or the community
The religion or political party
Institution or the industry
Whatever the race or the country
Whatever the thing or whoever the one
In the visible and invisible world

Everywhere and anywhere life exists
When Love generation does not persist
Human lives degenerate as we can easily see
Because the 'centre cannot hold' with ease—-
There are given ways for love expressions
Geared towards progress and order in Creation
For the maintenance of peace and harmony
On earth as done in heaven

Governed by the cardinal rule
"Do unto others as should be done to you"
This virtue and many others
Is God's nurturing mantra
To be sustained in all our chakras
For sharing His universal gifts of arms
Alas! in the world today we are deluged
With backlashes of the loss of these virtues

Creation works with versatile hands
All the virtues are God's midwifery hands
Without them all in unceasing operation
The 'delivery' of Love suffers complications
And all life become compromised
Let us now stop rejecting our own nature
And the use of the protective measures
Meant to prevent all harmful departures

The measures abound in all the virtues
That encompass all benevolent values
TOLERANCE speaks to it
In living and letting others live
Not frustrating nor inhibiting
Not discriminating but unifying
Not suppressing but emancipating
Not oppressing but liberating

GENEROSITY speaks to it
In the act of giving
Wanting to share one's blessings
For the good and benefit of others

In kind or in other ways that matter
Implementing God's Creations edict
For necessary balance and equity
Sharing all His wealth equally

His Air we breathe is equally shared
His lands we live on and cultivate
Equally given to all earth's inmates
His sun does not discriminate
On whom its rays may embrace
Nor who may need a shade
His moon does not discriminate
On who may see its rays

Night falls for everyone
The day breaks for everyone
The stars twinkle for everyone
The storms rage at the rich and the poor
The rain falls on palaces and huts
His life force is given to everyone
All nature obey His laws of life

So to live man must comply
Selfishness is unnatural
For it is insecurity bred
And possessiveness fed
It opposes natural virtuous giving
Implanting corrupting bribing
Ignoring the examples nature has set
For us to emulate
In order to ride on good fortune's train

HONESTY is another lost virtue
Seldom in application in this spiritual school
We misrepresent matters to suit our moods
Lie and fabricate events and causes too
Using service to country as a ruse
In many occasions we go to war
Kill and maim our fellowmen all
In violation of the law of Love

We claim false values of our products
Exaggerate the efficacy of our drugs
The performances of our inventions and stunts
The nutritional values of the food brands we sell
Disguise our intention at given events
Falsify our identities in many kinds of documents
Give false testimonies even under oath
All in violation of the honesty code

PATIENCE and PERSEVERANCE are Siamese twins
Supporting our abilities to maintain our grips
On events that challenge our talents and wits
Doubling our chances with increased hope
Of achieving successes in any role
No matter what the circumstances may be
Unfortunately much good remains to be seen
For our rancour with Love keeps progress in chains

To be patient is a virtue as ever said
Meant for equanimity and confidence in self
So to continue a course of action
And conclude it in spite of all obstructions

Not prospecting for failure or success
Patience as a virtue has thrown up her hands too
Staring at human beings pushing scoops
Of dangerous chemicals down their throats for food

DILIGENCE lies in our being persistent
Carefully engaged and consistent
Drilling our skills till the end of any project
KINDNESS and COMPASSION fulfil the prospect
Of harnessing and sustaining peace and progress
They are meant to prompt sensitivity to others needs
We all have fellow feelings
We all need someone caring

In Creation we cannot stand alone
In Creation God gave us the code
In the symbioses of all that is manifest
The earth and the heavens interact
Land and water are in a pact
Males and females come together
Man and woman magnetise each other
For the perpetuation of the human race

We are expected to express this gift of grace
Which prompts us to empathise and help
So all hands will be on deck
In the upbuilding of Creation
And the welfare of all nations
To be kind and compassionate
Was to arrest suffering and desolation
Of all dwellers amidst opulent Creation

Like father like son
Like Creator like creatures
With helpful intention He spreads His treasures
To all dwellers in His mansions
Showing us the way that we must function
To give help is the magic wand
That filled primordial void with wonderful forms
We came out of Help to continue the Helping...

LOYALTY another virtue given to us
Requires us to stand up for causes
That uplift mankind of any breed
Unswervingly supporting benevolent schemes
For all in Creation, both man and beast
FAITHFULNESS and FIDELITY take the lead
In keeping us on course as we steer the wheels
Of integrity in all relationships

JUSTICE entrenched in the Will of Holy Love
Whips the cain of fairness
In all man's actions and interactions
Maintaining balance and sublime peace
In the ramified mechanisms of Creation
For the smooth running of all nations
Eliminating the possibility of frictions
Forestalling all complications and repercussions

We are endowed with many other virtues
All meant to maintain life's good values
Pilot us on the paths of benevolence
Shine the light of uprightness

Ensure harmony and uninhibited progress
In all aspects of human endeavour
SINCERITY and HONESTY make sure
What we say is what we mean

To avoid confusion in all creeds
Allay misunderstanding of our intensions
Rule out inconsistencies in our transactions
Build unwavering confidence in each other
Instil trust and reliability in each other
Uphold human integrity
Avoid anger and hostility
Above all to forestall prejudices

PURITY and CHASTITY are unattainable in their sublimity
But manifest in faithfulness and sincerity
Maintained in moral uprightness
Keeping humanity's integrity unsoiled
Their values unadulterated, uncorrupted
Sanitising causes embarked upon
Adorning the robe of genuineness
In the catwalks of life

The virtue of SERENITY opens the door to confidence
It dances with challenges
And quells the storms of irritability
It subdues forces of oppositions
It bathes man with water of ablution
It puts stress and strife to bed
It serenades our hearts
Like the giggling of rippling waters

It is meant to help us take things in our stride
To subjugate all fears and strife
When things deviate from our expectations
But to trust our intuitions
Because we have the requisite abilities
Bequeathed in benevolent sublimity
To every member of the human society
To achieve success in all activities

HUMILITY goes hand in hand with CIVILITY
They ensure peace and tranquility
And see to it that we respect
And value everyone alive
Humility curbs aggression
And gives the ego a gentle civil mane
It propagates kindness
And makes all deeds sane

Humility curbs vanity
It restrains sagacity and ferocity
It prevents arrogation of power to self
It guards against egotism
Which brews antagonism
And disregards the notion of altruism
The humble is unpretentious
He or she is always very cautious

He or she is courteous
To such all life is precious
No matter the race
Whatever the case

Cause all deserve respect
For the contribution they are to make
For mankind's sake
That's all it takes to make us all safe

In humility's forbearing trail
Comes the sense of SHAME
A virtue now put to shame
A virtue now disdained
A restraining gift now shunned
By most in the bid for fame
For male and female it is the same
We all are to be blamed

For the decadence that reigns
Since we lost our senses of shame
Shyness was given to all mankind
To help us live with honour that is sublime
But obsession with sex, money and glamour
Has brewed a shameless culture
Which promotes moral dementia
Steeped in recurring spiritual inertia

H.   Born To Love

Let us remember
We are born Colour blind
To live colour blind
So let us therefore live Colour blind
We are born Status blind
To live Status blind
So let us therefore live Status blind
We are born discrimination blind

To live discrimination blind
So let us then live discrimination blind
We are born Looks blind
To live Looks blind
So let us then live Looks blind
We are born Nationality blind
To live Nationality blind
So let us then live Nationality blind

We are born Religion blind
To live Religion blind
So let us live spiritually but Religion blind
We are born Race blind
To live Race blind
So let us live Race blind
We are born Inherently intuitive
So let us then listen to our small voices

To guide us only in Love's paths
We are born Inherently gregarious
So let us love to live together
We are born Inherently gracious
So let us live with grace and magnanimity
We are born Inherently positive
To live positively
So let us live our lives with positivity

We are born Undeniably imitative
To express Love through imitation
Let's make our lives exemplary
We are born Inherently social
To interact with love and joy
So let us live with love and joy
We are born Inherently kind
To live our lives with kindness

So let us live our lives with kindness
We are Naturally curious
To explore and understand Creation
And know what is and isn't true
So let us open our minds and spirits
To the tutoring powers of God's Love
To teach us what we need to know
And what we need not to know

We are Naturally adventurous
To find different pieces of the puzzle of life
So let us open the door of our hearts
To welcome all what are in God's Love file

And no more be constrained or paralysed
By fear or hate or war or phobias
No more be burdened by wrong choices
Sprung from blind lovelessness

Nor from callous political tricks and whims
For we will be free of all negative kinks
We are Naturally inventive
To give our gifts to the world
Of that which we were meant to contribute
In furthering the development of all humanity
We are Naturally creative
To give expressions of our talents to the world

I. The Immoral Explosions

Woman above all has lost her divination role
In the uncouth game of strip and show
Making her a play toy with no soul
Stuffed with mouthwatering sex treats
Dancing to the male like a puppet on a string
The priceless priestess reduced to a clown
In a world that has thrown away her crown
Fouling her saintly brows

In a world without the sense of shame
Bringing her down from her throne
Clouding her sacred sight and role
Making her a mouse in a cage of cats
Devouring her piece by piece, flesh by flesh
With dripping mouthfuls of gushing lust
Befogging the world with infectious dusts
Arising from her spiritual crash

Turning decorum into trash
In a world without the sense of shame
The word sexy is now the mantra
In all circles of the modern man and modern woman
Speaking in the gibberish tongue
Of the confused permissive throng
Men too, spare nothing in their bid to compete
In the greed of the decadent feasts

In a world without Love and the sense of shame
Stripping and showing their all and all
To complete the spiritual downfall
Leading to indecent behaviours
Indecent vogues and fashions for all
Levity looming and glaring everywhere
Here, there, no matter where
In a world without Love and the sense of shame

J. *Need For Change*

Everyone needs and wants to succeed
Love alone is our shield in this field
It fights and defeats all the challenges we meet
Through thick and thin in the world we live
Making our words, thoughts and actions
Comply with The Divine Love injunctions
Is the secure armour for winning all the wars
For lasting peace in our beleaguered world

All the happenings in our world today
Strike apprehensive fearful chords
In the psyche of discerning human minds
In response to the dangerous signs
Of the prevalent proclivity
To crass moral depravity
Putting man on the edge
No matter the age

Cause Love's vibrations in our every cell
Propel all actions of Love to success
Without such actions we crawl in grime
And blame God for our miserable plights
But remember He gave us the free will
Right from the very beginning
The free will to exploit His treasure troves
And reap whatever we sow!

But we have vandalised and scandalised
Confounded and complicated
Corrupted and sabotaged
Our own prospects of survival
In a battling world of jackals
Clad in fake human overalls
Not the "likeness of the Image of God"
But the likenesses of our own images

Roaming the earth with intentions
And behaviours that defy comprehension
But, we can arrest the acceleration
Of this terrible decline
Reaffirm and reclaim our noble birthrights
Rise with Love to boldly salvage
The sublime privileges
We have callously ravaged

We owe it to ourselves
To regain our envious spiritual place
As those truly made in the likeness
Of the Image of the Living God
Applying our sacred loving mights
To fight and win the survival fight
Do our best to sanitise and sanctify
All what we say, think and do

In politics, religion and the society too
To win the battle for Love now afoot
By making all the Virtues manifest
In our offices and industries

In our homes and communities
Anywhere that we may be
In our kitchens
Or when we go fishing

In our studios or patios socialising
Anywhere humans live or congregate
In all our stores, booths and stalls
Sitting in the crowd or alone by the shores
Serving or being served in our clubs
In our hospitals
Or in our cubicles
In our factories

Or in our dormitories
In our schools or by the pools
By the furnaces
Or in the forest
In the government
Or in entertainment
In law enactment and enforcement
Or in our public and social lives

In relationships of any kind
In interaction with all the tribes
With all the Jews and all the Gentiles
All the birds and all the insects
All the trees in the jungles and forests
All the animals and the reptiles
In the daytime or at nighttime
In the remotest parts of the world

With all the stones and the rocks
With all the waters in the rivers
With the air and the frozen winter
The storms and the breeze
And the cold that makes things freeze
With the Earth and the sun
The moon at night and the stars above
That give us light by twinkling in at night

The virtues will help us win the fight
In whatever stress and whatever plight
They rap at the door of our hearts
For us to let them in
To give us the support we need
To change our hearts to Love for all
At work or play whatever is at play
At night or day they don't complain

They make all the rules fair
Even when we are cooking
They bid us make the meals healthy
When we are eating
They prompt us to avoid overeating
When we are shopping
They enable us to be frugal
All in all, the virtues make us truly human

They are canes for our support on rough lands
They are flash lights to illuminate our paths
They are weapons with which to fight and win
The battle between right and wrong, good and evil

They protect us against any storm
To succeed and never face defeat or loss
They are like boats to cross all raging seas
They are reliable friends in all our daily deeds

They are meant for solving the puzzles
Of all man's bewildering tussles
Theories suffocate each other
In our world's literary arenas
Analysed and argued exhaustively
In our world's academic seminars
Groups and organisations abound
Posing to turn the situation around

Yet from millennia to millennia
Our phobias and hysterias
Increase in leaps and bounds
Peace has not yet been found
Base pursuits highjacking our lives
From morning till night we drive
Each other mad with short sights
Ignoring each other's plight

Because Love the mother of all virtues
Has not yet become our way, the only way
The rich gets richer
Because of lack of Love for all
The poor gets poorer
Because of lack of Love for all
We get more immoral
because of lack of Love for all

We get more material
Because of lack of Love for all
Wars and suffering escalate
Because of lack of love for all
Charities fail to break the chain
Because of lack of true love for all
Self-interest propelling the schemes
And handouts never substituting self esteem

As we speak
All our vices still increase
In spite of missionaries round the world
Human lives are lost in the suffocating fog
All efforts at all levels have been to no avail
Politics and religion have not prevailed
Their tactics and doctrines till date
Have much to explain in this travail

Is it any wonder many may ponder
Why all nations are so torn asunder
Facing the charge of civic stormy weather
Threatening mankind from east and west
From the north and the south
There is no more room now for playing games
All our excuses have been proven lame
Beleaguered mankind has to make a choice

Between greed and Love
Between hate and Love
For nature wants to return our boomerangs
Engraved with 'Living Love now and always'

Love is the faithful answer to all our problems
Love for everyone and everything in Creation
Because everything is Love
And Love truly conquers all

K. Living Is Loving

To truly live is to Love
Cause we breath Love
We eat Love
We drink Love
All around us is of Love
All above us is of Love
All within us is of Love
All that keep us alive come from Love

Let's therefore turn to Love cause it is sufficient
Let's therefore turn to Love cause it's efficient
In making the world a liveable place
We may be black
We may be white
We may be brown and all the rest
No matter what is our race
Our earth is a magnanimous treasure chest

That for ever returns abundant yields
Of every single planted seed
A world that gives back all what it takes
If we plant Love we will reap more love
But if we plant hatred
We will reap more hatred
Which one do we choose to reap
If not the yields of our sown Loving seeds

We may be believers or disbeliever
Atheists, agnostics or resisters
We may be Buddhists or Muslims
Christians, Jews or Hindus
Pagans or of other persuasions
Prompting certain ideologies and passions
That conflict with one another
Creating rancour not joy in a world of Love

None of us was born an atheist
None of us was born an agnostic
None of us was born a Christian
None a Jew, a Hindu or a Buddhist
Neither a medicine man or a Muslim
All the above are acquired faiths
To enable us navigate through our intriguing world
Some are popular some are not

The faith we acquire does the best
If it helps us remember the original plan
Stored in our glands
To conduct our biological bands
In the expression of Love with all our body parts
Love is in all our glands
The tonic God has given to man
For fortifying our bids for progress

We are all born with eyes to see with Love
We are all born with mouths to eat with Love
Tongues to speak with Love
Brains to think with Love

Hearts to feel with Love
Hands and feet to perform with Love
All our other body parts to do the same
Our DNAs eulogies our oneness in Love
As God's Love dutiful agent
Our world gives back what it receives
Perpetual Love is what it receives
It gives back perpetuating Living Love

To perpetuate the Love that have taken many forms
In a world made from the energy of Love
Cause like perpetuates its own likes
And Love perpetuates Love!
In this perpetuating role
The earth giving back what it has
As farmers in earth's farm lands
When we sow grains

The earth gives back abundant grains
So if we want rice
We must plant rice
For the earth to give back abundant rice
If we want joy
We need to give joy
To make the earth resound with joy
If we want peace

We need to make peace
To make the earth return lasting peace
If we want kindness to do the same
So the earth will be kind to all men

If we want to be Loved
We need to give Love to all
So to enjoy the Love we share
In the Love returned by all the world
In the law of reciprocity
The law of homogeneity
The law of gravity
In the cardinal law of Love for all

So let us love to quell all feuds
Political, religious, and cultural
Social, racial and ethical,
Intellectual, agricultural and industrial,
Medical, mental and physical
All areas of our daily lives
Can only have beneficial vibes
If conducted with nothing but the baton of LOVE

Is Enough Not Enough?

If the taste of the pudding
Is truly in the eating
And seeing believing
Have we not fought enough WARS round the globe
Resulting from GREED round the globe
Resulting from OPPRESSION round the globe
Resulting from RACISM round the globe
Resulting from AGGRESSION round the globe

Resulting from POWER ABUSE in a world of Love
Have we not seen enough KILLINGS in a world of Love
Resulting from JEALOUSY in a world of Love.
Resulting from HATRED in a world of Love
Resulting from WANT in a world of Love
Resulting from CRUELTY in a world of Love
Resulting from FALSE CLAIMS in a world of Love
Resulting from INSENSITIVITY in a world of Love

Have we not witnessed enough HYPOCRISY
Participated enough in LYING
Participated enough in DECEIVING
Participated enough in MALIGNING
Participated enough in CONSPIRING
Enough in CONNIVING
Enough in CRITICISING
Enough in DEGRADING

Have we not participated enough in not GIVING
Enough in not FORGIVING
Enough in not RESPECTING
Enough in not SACRIFICING
Enough in bullying or terrorising
Enough in not being HONEST
Enough in being COMPLACENT
Enough In IGNORING OUR OWN TRUE NATURE!

With Love held hostage within its own body
Bound and gagged by its own guardian
Restrained and chained in perpetual house arrest
Given limited exposure and expressions
In the milieu of human interactions
Forcing it to lose its ability
To serve its Maker above
With persistent ministry of Love to all

America is a glimpse to a new world
A torchbearer of a sacred dream
Where all the races of the evolving world
Are brought to be together
By choice or not for the Divine agenda
Of creating a gathering of all humanity
Living together in perfect harmony
Practicing the laws of Living Love

With one neighbour and another
One citizen and another
Each being his brother's keeper
Loving him as he loves himself

Our Leaders and us have been saboteurs
Of this sacred corrective measure
Proudly desecrating our gifts
Multiplying all the foregoing ills

In the perpetration of the same deeds
That keep us from fulfilling the sacred dream
Of standing with our flags raised
To the shining nation on the hill
Pride of distorted patriotism
Fanned by vanity and egotism
Have spun the vision to an illusion
And the illusion to delusion

We claim the trophies for the achievements
Of the assembled global talents
Wearing the glories on our national sleeves
But the real dream can only come true
If we all live by the Law of Love
Which will ensure that everyone alive
Will come to know what it takes
To make the world a better place for all

Enough Is Enough

As dual entities walking on earth
Made of invisible spirit and visible flesh
The former ethereal the latter gross material
The former invisible the latter corporeal
The former immortal the latter mortal
Both suffering same abuses
The visible abuses have visibly reduced
Our world of Love into a world of no Love

The invisible results from our visible faults
Harnessed by the invisible forces
Of our metaphysical world
Doubly affecting our lives here
And our lives after here
Our responsibilities are doubly grave
We therefore cannot easily escape
The backlash even after the grave

So let us take serious look around
And notice how seriously profound
The acts we commit day and night
And all what we say think and hide
Have impacted the fruits of our lives
As politicians and civilians
Parents and guardians
Corporate heads and investors

Doctors and nurses
Scientists and artist
Queens and Kings
Religious heads and drones
Bishops and Popes
Haves and have nots
The employee and the boss
Educators and innovators

Clouds of dark emissions
Spouted from our Loveless transactions
Without due consideration of their effects
On our environments and our humanity
Transmitted on one hand personally
Or with the aid of advanced technology
And on the other hand
By the invisible forces of creation

With more sublime profundity
In the dual operation of the mortal man
And his immortal spirit, have combined
To create the bed we must now willy-nilly lie
To harvest the confounding fruits quite ripe
Of the compromising hybrids
Of sacred germs with none-sacred seeds
In the bid for progress by any means

This ticking bomb in world affairs
Triggered by all the ills that we have bred
With wrong policies in our politics and ethics
Hold us captive and apprehensive

The politicians of the world
Aided and abetted by bigotry
Amplified by questionable histories
Backed by false claims and counter claims

Of power and unrivalled fame
Forged in the flames of bewildering greed
Have turned our hearts to steel
Have made us slow to prove
That we are not to be taken for fools
That we are human beings
Who still have feelings
Of some shame and gnawing pains

Of lost humanity and integrity
Of knowing failure and adversity
Of feeling no one is on the people's side
No one wants to help the people rise
From the skeletons we have become
Because of famines caused by wars
Between one nation and another
No one cares if we lose our rights

And care less even if we die
From bullets from the gangs
Or from bombs from war tanks
Let alone from hunger pangs
Or from the daily hammering rains
That carry away our remains
And our survivors without roofs o'er their heads
Roaming hopelessly with their lives on hold

No one treating the suppurating sores
That now cover mankind from head to toe
With the endemic wounds inflicted by mankind's foe
Of hopelessness from LOVELESSNESS!...
Only Living Love can bring the change we need
In the adamantine Will of GOD
Only Living Love in all its ramifications
Can turn our fate around...

The leaders of our world
Are the totem poles of our harrowing past
The in-scripted whirling boomerangs
Returning to all the launchers hands
To make us come to terms with reality
And discern with all clarity
What HATE is and what LOVE is not
What makes us truly human and what does not

What should endure and what should not
The road we should tread from now on
The road we should abandon from this day on
The choice we should make to win the noble fight
Between what is wrong and what is proven right
In the eyes of God therefore that of man
In all the land
And fields of Life

Our heads of states are the boomerangs
Branded with images with our own hands
The towering totem poles in the gaze of the world
The overall symbols of our hopes and dreams

For better fates in our survival drills
Hopes that have never been sustained
Dreams that have never been attained
Despite our fierce religious and political games

By definition in politicking
What is often done is whitewashing
Policies that are "seemingly sensible
And judicious under the circumstances"
Not indisputably sensible
Under all circumstances
On the just principles of Divine Love
De-emphasising political ideologies

And the enforcement of loveless policies
But affirming constant expressions
Of practical Living Love
To achieve the elusive goal
For it is equipped to conquer everything
That challenge all humanity
Physically or emotionally
Materially or spiritually

Reflection

So, armed with the power of Living Love
Let's pair ourselves with Donald Trump
Which one of us can truly say
That we love others as we love ourselves?
If he says he doesn't and we say we don't
Then how can we share the Love
Meant for one and all mankind
As those made in the likeness of God's Image?

Armed with the power of Living Love
Let's pair ourselves with heads of states
Which one of us can truly say
That we do to others as we would want done to us?
If they say they don't and we say we don't
Then how can we advance a world of kindness
A world of empathy and mutual respect
Showing we are our brothers' keepers?

Armed with the power of Love
Let's pair ourselves with heads of states
Which one of us can easily say
That we tell the truth both night and day? If
they say they can't and we say we can't Then
how can we promote an honest world
Where everyone's yea remains yea
And everyone's nay remains nay?

Armed with the power of Living Love
Let's pair ourselves with heads of states
Which one of us can easily claim
To readily forgive our offenders?
If they say they cannot and we say we can't
Then how can our debts be forgiven
And our wrongs be stricken off in heaven
When we fail to forgive our debtors here on earth?

Armed with the power of Love
Let's pair ourselves with heads of states
Which one of us can easily say
That we are not greedy and self-centred?
If they say they cannot and we say the same
Then how can we both help
To build a world where everyone shares
The abundance of nature's wealth?

Feeling content with what we have
Ridding the world of greed's laden bags
That have led to wars and insurrection
Holocausts, genocides and homicides
Let's pair ourselves with our world leaders
Which one of us can easily say
We give Helping hands with no strings attached
In kind or money or in any other form?

If they say they can't and we say we can't
Then how can we help to create a kind world
Armed with the power of Love
To create heaven on earth?

Let's pair ourselves with our world leaders
Which one of us can easily say
That we are not racist
Nor are we divisive?

If they say they cannot and we say the same
Then how can we erase prejudice in our world?
How can we bury discrimination in our world?
How can we ever have peace in our world?
How can we eliminate hypocrisy in our world?
How can we have equity in our world?
How can we ever have justice in our world
If we cannot stand as one in God's Love?

Charity Begins At Home

Charity begins at home
Let Love Be and Lead the Way at home
In everything we do everyday
From the beginning till the end of the day
To activate all the attributes
Of Love within the spirit of every child
That he or she may be fully armed
To embrace the world with open arms

Let Love Be and Lead the Way
In all our communities every day
The active Love will eradicate
All crimes and all adversaries
Create peace and camaraderie
Sharing all our gifts with one another
Trusting all with our lives in any weather
Ridding us of fear of one another

Let Love Be and Lead the way
The practice of the activated Love
In businesses and industries everyday
Will eradicate greed and exploitation
Aggrandisement and deception
Dispossession of the have nots
For the benefit of the have much
Which leads to economic blackballs

Let Love Be and Lead the way
In governance everywhere
To grant equality and justice to all
Implement policies that benefit all
Eliminate hypocrisy and bigotry
Create opportunities for the good of all
No matter from where they may come
No matter the race into which they are born

Let Love Be and Lead the way everywhere
To eradicate our throes and woes right away
Let hunger and want rest in peace
Cast violence and aggression down the precipice
Lock torture and oppression in an eternal jail
And set peace and compassion free to rein
At last with the power of eternal Love
That transforms and protects all

Let Love Be and Lead the Way
In our law enforcement systems everywhere
Run megalomania and intimidation out of town
And let justice with kindness wear the crown
Of true humanity
Not parading sheer cruelty
But empowering the people
Meant to be served with Love

Let Love Be and Lead the Way
In our societies everywhere
To drive poverty far away
And share the wealth God gave

To all the inhabitants of the earth
Driving all handout away
Cremating national debts and insolvency
Despondency and dependency

Let Love Be and Lead the Way
In our lives everywhere
Eliminating fear and distress
Spreading peace and happiness
Throughout the existing continents
Let Love Be and Lead the Way
In our lives everywhere
To harmonise with God's loving ways

Let Love Be and Lead the Way
In everything we do everywhere
No matter who we are
No matter what we are
No matter where we've been
No matter where we want to be
No matter our creed
Nor our where with all

Let Love Be and Lead the Way
In everything we do every day
From childhood to adulthood
From the adventurous youths
To the accomplished groom
From the starry-eyed dreamer
To the Corporate employer
The mentor and benefactor

Giving to our fellow men
The Love we all receive everyday
Every hour and every split second of the day
From the Lord of all creation
God the Father Almighty
The Creator of the universe
OMNISCIENT, OMNIPRESENT, OMNIPOTENT
For all eternity!

Let Love Lead and Be The Only Way
So that Wars will be no more
Let Love be and lead the way
So that TERRORISM will be no more
Let Love be and lead the way
So that POVERTY will be no more
Let Love be and lead the way
So that MURDERS will be no more

Let Love be and lead the way
So that CRIMES will be no more
Let Love be and lead the way
So that CORRUPTION will be no more
Let Love be and lead the way
So that RACISM will be no more
Let Love be and lead the way
So that HATRED will be no more

Let Love be and lead the way
So that PREJUDICE will be no more
Let Love be and lead the way
So that GREED will be no more

Let Love be and lead the way
So that EXPLOITATION will be no more
Let Love be and lead the way
So that EGOTISM will be no more

Let Love be and lead the way
So that NEPOTISM will be no more
Let Love be and lead the way
So that DESPOTISM will be no more
Let Love be and lead the way
So that DICTATORSHIP will be no more
Let Love be and lead the way
So that GENOCIDES will be no more
And peace will reign everywhere in the world

Epilogue

Our leaders paint high definition portraits
Of skeletons in their and all mankind's closets
Let us now put the tale-tell bones to rest
That our world may be free of their spells
That's why Donald Trump ———
It's not enough to castigate the likes of him
It's not enough to deride the likes of him
It's not enough to emulate the likes of him

Nor enough to defend the likes of him
Cause the light of Love shines on us all
That we may see our own faults in him
With the lens of God's universal eye ofLove
Knowing that the tsunamis of our lovelessness
The hurricanes of our lovelessness
The cyclones and tornadoes of our lovelessness
All other catastrophes of our lovelessness

Are nature's ways of shaking off
The pollution from our lovelessness
And wake us up to ask why
We have turned our backs on who we really are
And what we are meant to be doing here
In all areas of life
From morn till night till the day we die
If not to manifest the fruits of Love

What we need for success in the fight
Is a change of heart to Loving all
Not a change of governments from fall to fall
What we need to succeed in the fight
Is a change of hearts to Loving all
Not a change of political parties fall tho fall
What we need to succeed in the fight
Is a change of hearts to Loving all

Not a change of the economy of the world
But the change of heart of every man in the world
To Love, universal Love!!!

THE PERVASIVENESS
OF SUBLIME LOVE

On a more personal note, let me share these experiences that I have had of the workings of the power of Love on levels that reveal the sublimity of and pervasiveness of its mechanism, demonstrating its universality in execution for the maintenance of harmony in this Creation that is governed only by the power of Love. I am sure you may have had some yourself.

I had a potted plant in Evanston Illinois, of blooming beautiful hibiscus in our living room. Every year its beauty was marred by disturbing pests of fruit flies that loved the nectar of the flowers. In my ignorance and concern, I bought Raids and angrily attacked the poor things to get rid of them. Indeed, they would die of the poison to my great relief that season but would promptly return in time in the next!

It took me three seasons of despair to then realise that I was going against the law of Love for my fellow creatures in our world. I had no right to take their lives. They too had the right to live and enjoy the gift from the benefactor, our God! So, I appealed to the loving nature beings that take care of all nature to handle the situation in accordance with the Will of the giver off all life. In exactly three days the pestering flies were gone and never came back again in any season!

At another occasion I was chatting with a neighbour by our apartment car park in Skokie, Illinois, two wasps came between us and menacingly buzzed around the neighbour who was frantically flapping and flagging at them to chase them away. I intervened and asked her to remain calm to dissipate the vibration of her fear and agitation which was disturbing the wasps sensing of the natural state of harmonious peace and Love that they understand.

She stopped her disturbing actions and the wasps finally swooped by me and buzzed away!

At another occasion, a group of us were clearing a bush for the building of our Temple of The Grail Movement in Atlanta. We paused for lunch sitting on a bench in the clearing. Behold a swarm of insects came rolling across forming a conical shape before us, and about three feet away and above us. I gently told them to withdraw into the interior of the forests where they would find adequate and suitable nourishment other than the ones we were having. They heard me because they promptly swung round back into the forest and out of sight.

Half an hour or so later, my co-crossbearer who was sitting next to me and saw the insects in the first encounter, nudged at me and said:

"Hey look, your friends have now gone to trouble the children at their lunch (sitting in the clearing ten feet on our right), better talk to them again and send them away from the children".

I promptly raised my voice and told them what I had said before. To our delight and gratitude, they did and never returned to trouble any of us again!

On the 23rd of November, 2018, a friend and I were waiting in someone's living room to be given a ride to a party. A young girl was trying to stop a medium size grey dog from coming at us. I asked the girl to let the dog be. The dog gingerly went to sniff at my friend sitting next to me on the sofa, then he or she turned to do the same to me. He/she repeated this action then came closer to me and raised its left paw and placed it gently on my right knee and looked up at me...

I have always loved animals and have had pets of guinea pigs, dogs and a parrot many years ago but don't now. So, I told the dog that I understood him as I stroked its head. Then it raised both fore-legs and gently placed them on my knees and looked at me, raising its head very close to my face. I held its head and stroked it, telling him I totally understood his gesture and shared its understanding of that which binds us all as creatures made with and driven by the energy and sublime power of God's Love for one another.

Love is the common denominator for all existence and the only power that can unite all mankind to live in harmony and peace with one another in the fulfilment of our common destiny!

Thank you all.